THE
FORTY WEEKS
LEADER'S
GUIDEBOOK

for
Parish Pastors,
Adult Faith Formation Directors,
RCIA, Campus Ministry,
Vocation Directors & Clergy and Deacon
Formation Coordinators

William M. Watson, SJ

Sacred Story Press
1401 E Jefferson St., STE 405
Seattle, WA 981222

Imprimi Potest
Rev. Scott R. Santarosa, SJ

Imprimatur
Very Rev. George V. Murry, SJ

DEDICATED TO
OUR LADY OF THE WAY

ISBN-13: 978-1507874004
ISBN-10: 1507874006

CONTENTS

There are very few who realize what

God would make of them if they abandoned

themselves entirely to His hands, and let themselves

be formed by His grace. A thick and shapeless

tree trunk would never believe that it could

become a statue, admired as a miracle of sculpture…

and would never consent to submit itself to

the chisel of the sculptor who, as St. Augustine says,

sees by his genius what he can make of it.

Many people who, we see, now scarcely

live as Christians, do not understand that

they could become saints, if they would let

themselves be formed by the grace of God,

if they did not ruin His plans by

resisting the work which He wants to do.

St. Ignatius Loyola

FOREWORD

The Ignatian Examen in the Third Millennium[1]

Gospel faith is necessarily linked to the needs of the poor and the powerless. Sin running through the center of human hearts disrupts not only our knowledge of God, but also our desire to care for others, especially the most disadvantaged. This spiritual blindness and sickness manifests in the glorification of the self, the desire for wealth, the seeking of worldly honors and the heart's unbending pride. Unattended, it constantly evolves in the horrors of war, insatiable greed, disrespect for life, ecological damage, injustice, and poverty.

Unless and until Original Sin's spiritual superstructures rooted in individual hearts and souls are targeted and disarmed, no sustainable peace or justice in Church or human society is possible. This is true no matter how organized, expansive and effective our social service networks become. The Second Vatican Council declared that human effort to achieve positive progress for the world is constantly "endangered by pride and inordinate self-love."[2] Both the language and the experience of the Council match Ignatius' life story and spiritual insights.

Awakening to spiritual *and* social realities—awakening to one's

---

[1] This section originally appeared as the Afterword in *Sacred Story: An Ignatian Examen for the Third Millennium*.

[2] *Gaudium et Spes*, § 37.

conscience and true human nature—are directly linked to the conversion process. Ignatius' foundational conversion after his wounding led to his *general examen* and his *night of the senses*. The social awakening he experienced on his pilgrimage to Montserrat allowed Ignatius to *see* the beggar who becomes a recipient of his support and care. But it was at the deeper, integrated level of conversion at Manresa that Ignatius was led to his *night of the spirit* and his *particular examen*. This deeper conversion according to Nadal is where Ignatius' desire to help souls was "born."[3]

This begins Ignatius' *Sacred Story.* He finds soldiers of a different sort to help build a company whose purpose his Constitutions declare is to "aid souls to reach their ultimate and supernatural end." The tools of his ministry founded on his progressive conversion are the *Spiritual Exercises* and the daily *Examen*. Both are aimed at helping individuals conquer self by uprooting inordinate attachments. For these spiritual pursuits Ignatius says are "the interior gifts which make those exterior means effective toward the end which is sought."[4]

Spiritual writers and theologians too often focus on Ignatius' mystical gifts. Those seeking the keys to his spiritual genius should focus instead on *when* he received his mystical gifts. It is only after he surrenders his life to God his Savior. The surrender of his will enables him to see himself, the world and God. It is only then that he says, "he felt as if he were another man with another mind."[5]

---

[3] Cusson Gilles Cusson, SJ, *Biblical Theology and the Spiritual Exercises*, trans. George Ganss, SJ, Mary Angela Roduit, RC (St. Louis: Institute of Jesuit Sources, 1988), 27. Cited hereafter as: "Cusson."

[4] *Constitutions of the Society of Jesus and Their Complimentary Norms*. Edited by John W. Padberg, SJ. St. Louis: Institute of Jesuit Sources *Part X*: § [813]—2.. Cited hereafter as *Constitutions*.

[5] Ganss, SJ, George E., and Parmananda R. Divarkar, SJ, Edward J. Malatesta, SJ, Martin

This is the tipping point of his history transforming his life from anti-story into a *Sacred Story*. He finally wakes up. No subsequent event or combination of events and graces will ever equal the rush of spiritual oxygen that renewed his mind and heart at this one moment in time. It was at that one moment in time that Ignatius saw himself, the world, and the kingdom of God, because he had been born from above (Jn 3:3). That one-third of the *Autobiography* is dedicated to these critical first two years of his conversion journey should catch our attention.

Ignatius manifests three fundamental fruits of the classical path of purgation and illumination that each of us in our own way need to imitate: (1) he honestly named his sins and surrendered his life to God, admitting he could not save himself; (2) in so doing, he woke to see both his life and the world through the eyes of God—in this clarity of vision and depth of understanding, Polanco says, he wept even more bitterly over the sins of his past life and;[6] (3) understanding Christ as his Savior and Lord, he submitted his will, allowing God to lead him to the fullness of his authentic identity—his *Sacred Story*.

The late Cardinal Carlo Martini discussed the contemporary crisis of faith using the symbol of the barren tree. He recognized signs of renewal in many places, but to him, sterility appeared more evident: meetings, congresses, programs, renewals, encounters, many beautiful words, and gilt facades behind which there is almost nothing. Where is the fruit? Churches, seminaries and novitiates are, in many cases, empty. Regarding the ratio of leaves and fruit in our individual Christian lives, he says:

Each one has to wonder how the Lord looks at our leaves, i.e., the

---

E. Palmer, SJ, *Ignatius of Loyola: The Spiritual Exercises and Selected Works* (Mahwah: Paulist Press, 1991), 81.

[6] Cusson, 27.

words, intentions, commitments, programs and little fruit, i.e., the ability to transmit the faith to others which, at its core, is the result, the ability to convert others, and to communicate the love of God, to give them life. Our gift of self to God is manifested in the ability to give to the other the spark of love for the Lord that He has placed within us. Here surely we must ask not only about the fruits, that God in his goodness allows us to gather, but also about the relationship between leaves and fruits, between what we might do and the actual reality of our lives.[7]

Martini's vision encompassed Europe. His insights can be applied equally to the entire Christian West. He invited us to look closely at our lives and the apostolates to which we dedicate our time and treasure. Do our efforts at evangelization, our works for justice, our thousands of hospitals, grade schools, high schools, universities and parishes produce fruit? Does the salt savor (Mt 5:13)? In the Ignatian world, do we have many leaves and little fruit? Are we cultivating and sharing the fruits of the spiritual tree entrusted to us? Are Ignatius' spiritual methods, and the treasures of integrated conversion they facilitate, underutilized or their potency blunted?

Ignatius' pre-conversion life mirrors our contemporary faith and cultural crises. Out of his dysfunction, Christ gives the Church one of its greatest saints. A new dynamic spirituality that meets head-on the greatest social, intellectual, moral, religious, human and

---

[7] "Si miramos a nuestro alrededor, ciertamente esta situación nos impresiona. Pero si después la aplicamos a nosotros mismos, de seguro cada uno tiene que preguntarse hasta qué punto el Señor ve en nosotros hojas, es decir, palabras, propósitos, compromisos, programas y poco fruto, es decir, *capacidad de transmitir a otros la fe*, que, en el fondo, es el fruto, capacidad de convertir a otros de comunicar el amor de Dios, de hacer que vivan. Nuestra autodonación. A Dios se manifiesta el la capacidad de dar también a otros aqeulla chispa de amor al Señor que Él ha puesto en nosotros. Aquí ciertamente hemos de preguntarnos no solo acerca de los frutos que el Señor en su bondad nos permite recoger, sino también *acerca de la relación* entre hojas y frutos, entre lo que podríamos hacer y lo que en realidad somos durante toda la vida." Martini, Cardinal Carlo Maria. *Los Ejercicios De San Ignacio a la luz del Evangelio de Mateo*: 2a edición (Bilbao, Desclée de Brouwer, 2008), 55-56.

psychological crises the Church has ever encountered is born. Paul VI understood the tremendous need of Ignatius' vibrant spirituality, especially in light of the crises facing the modern world:

You have a spirituality strongly traced out, an unequivocal identity and a centuries-old confirmation which is based on the validity of methods, which, having passed through the crucible of history, still bear the imprint of the strong spirit of St. Ignatius...You are at the head of that interior renewal which the Church is facing in this secularized world, especially after the Second Vatican Council. Your Society, is we say, the test of the validity of the Church throughout the centuries; it is perhaps one of the most meaningful crucibles in which are encountered the difficulties, the temptations, the efforts, the perpetuity and the successes of the whole Church.[8]

Ignatius' life, conversion and spiritual legacy are needed now more than ever. But the integrity of Ignatius' spiritual disciplines to promote integrated growth must be protected and their potency nurtured. There are temptations on all sides. Early on, the Inquisition prevented St. Ignatius from "helping souls" by prohibiting him from defining sin. We must be vigilant in our own day and not make their same mistake. Ignatian Spirituality, in its various methods including the *Examens,* must help souls properly identify sin. This is especially true at the foundational stage of conversion.

But evangelization must break the stalemate between arrogance and timidity. Evangelization that relies principally on the proclamation of laws and boundaries with little mercy is the Phariseeism condemned by Christ. Evangelization with no laws or boundaries except a bending, evolving definition of truth merely

---

[8] *Jesuit Life and Mission Today: The Decrees & Accompanying Documents of the 31st-35th General Congregations of the Society of Jesus.* Edited by John W. Padberg, SJ. St. Louis: Institute of Jesuit Sources, 384.

sanctions the individualist's desires and the narcissist's demands. Both methods are ultimately impotent and unsustainable and have been denounced by Pope Francis.[9]

Success for the Church's evangelization is achievable along the narrow path of God's mercy and justice. Mercy is indispensable for humanity's sufferings caused by the mortal damage to human nature in the Original Sin. And God's justice is that very same love in the form of boundaries protecting the created order and the distinctiveness of our human nature crafted in the image and likeness of God. When we evangelize with both mercy and justice, we help people find their way back to God and in freedom, serve the Kingdom—living life as a *Sacred Story*.

---

[9] - One, a temptation to hostile inflexibility, that is, wanting to close oneself within the written word, (the letter) and not allowing oneself to be surprised by God, by the God of surprises, (the spirit); within the law, within the certitude of what we know and not of what we still need to learn and to achieve. From the time of Christ, it is the temptation of the zealous, of the scrupulous, of the solicitous and of the so-called – today – "traditionalists" and also of the intellectuals.

- The temptation to a destructive tendency to goodness [it. buonismo], that in the name of a deceptive mercy binds the wounds without first curing them and treating them; that treats the symptoms and not the causes and the roots. It is the temptation of the "do-gooders," of the fearful, and also of the so-called "progressives and liberals."

- The temptation to transform stones into bread to break the long, heavy, and painful fast (cf. Lk 4:1-4); and also to transform the bread into a stone and cast it against the sinners, the weak, and the sick (cf Jn 8:7), that is, to transform it into unbearable burdens (Lk 11:46).

- The temptation to come down off the Cross, to please the people, and not stay there, in order to fulfil the will of the Father; to bow down to a worldly spirit instead of purifying it and bending it to the Spirit of God.

- The temptation to neglect the "*depositum fidei*" [the deposit of faith], not thinking of themselves as guardians but as owners or masters [of it]; or, on the other hand, the temptation to neglect reality, making use of meticulous language and a language of smoothing to say so many things and to say nothing! They call them "byzantinisms," I think, these things...

Dear brothers and sisters, the temptations must not frighten or disconcert us, or even discourage us, because no disciple is greater than his master; so if Jesus Himself was tempted – and even called Beelzebul (cf. Mt 12:24) – His disciples should not expect better treatment. (From Vatican Radio's provisional translation of Pope Francis' address to the Synod Fathers.)

This interior freedom for service is the hallmark of Ignatian Spirituality and the goal of *Sacred Story*. Ignatius' practice of the daily *Examen*, and the interior freedom it brought him, changed the history of the Church and the world. Imagine what a handful of people in every religious community, parish, high school and university around the earth could accomplish by living it daily.

William Watson, S.J.
January 1, 2015
Solemnity of Mary Mother of God

INTRODUCTION

We provide these resources to help you find the most fruitful avenues with *Forty Weeks: An Ignatian Path to Christ with Sacred Story Prayer*, in whatever ministries you guide or direct. The *Forty Weeks* book was designed to be a self-directed prayer journey that can be experienced by an individual Catholic or Christian seeking a more personal connection with Christ in daily life. *Forty Weeks* is also designed to be used in group settings for parish renewal, RCIA, Campus Ministry and other adult faith formation evangelization efforts in your Catholic or Christian communities.

Up to this point, most people have experienced Ignatian Spirituality through the Spiritual Exercises in a retreat setting or in the format known as the 19th Annotation. The latter is a form of doing the Exercises over a thirty-plus week period, seeing a spiritual director weekly or monthly and also engaging in group faith reflection activities. Programs for the 19th Annotation are commonly known by the name SEEL (Spiritual Exercises in Everyday Life).

For those familiar with Ignatian Spirituality, the *Examen* prayer that inspires *Forty Weeks* will be very familiar. The *Examen* is the most portable version of the dynamics that form *Spiritual Exercises*—a sort of *Spiritual Exercises* in miniature. This *Examen* method in *Forty Weeks* has three principal goals. First, to teach individuals how to see their lives holistically.

We all are aided in our spiritual journey when we understand how sin and dysfunction operate in our history to undermine God's plans for our happiness and well-being. Similar to Ignatius' *Spiritual Exercises*, this first goal of *Forty Weeks* seeks to help one honestly name sin, addiction and dysfunction in one's history and bring it to Christ, the Divine Physician, for healing in Sacramental Reconciliation. As such, it teaches one how to make Sacramental Reconciliation a regular and fruitful part of one's spiritual health regimen.

The second goal of *Forty Weeks* is to build a daily, personal relationship with Christ Jesus using the *Sacred Story Examen* method. Linked to the second goal, the third goal is learning how to discern the two different spiritual inspirations that are constantly working behind our conscious awareness—one pulling us toward the light, blessing and life; and the other, pulling us toward the darkness, curse and death. To draw closer to Christ in a daily, prayerful relationship demands that one develop a discerning heart. Goals two and three both require quiet restful periods of prayer for fifteen minutes, once or twice daily.

Thus, these three goals of *Forty Weeks* can form the basis of any parish renewal program; be a powerful supplement to an RCIA journey; help young adults in a college campus ministry setting learn how to grow into a mature faith; and/or be part of many different adult faith formation programs.

A Special Note to Pastors:

We have discovered with our work in multiple parishes in the Archdiocese of Seattle that the involvement of the pastor in the *Forty Weeks* process is vital for its long-term fruitfulness.

The pastor does not necessarily have to do the *Forty Weeks* program with his parishioners. However, those who have experienced its graces do become convinced of its power and want to share it with their flock.

However, it will make your program very, very effective if the pastor can offer some weekly encouragement to the group(s) making the journey (a comment at the end of Sunday Mass; a note in the weekly bulletin or a message on the parish website; a prayer in the Prayers of the Faithful on Sundays, a prayerful encouragement at a faith-sharing group meeting monthly; etc.).

Parishioners do follow the lead of the pastor and how you support those making this serious engagement with their faith is important. I strongly believe that if pastors prayerfully support those making this journey, the benefit will be the 30, 60, and 100 fold Jesus promised in the Scriptures.

This program is a school of prayer and a pathway to reconciliation and spiritual discernment. It is a way to meet Jesus personally each day of your life. The more people who annually make this journey, the more dynamic your parish will become. You will have more volunteers, more support and more will want to join a community whose individuals know Christ personally and share his message with others.

We are all being called by the New Evangelization to make our faith evident to the world. *Forty Weeks* can be great help in your local faith community. It is a program that will grow annually and in 3-5 years, your community will be transformed.

ോ

I

THE BASICS: PREPARATION AND LAUNCH

GETTING STARTED

Discipleship: *Forty Weeks' Sacred Story* Prayer

Many dioceses and parishes search for ways to promote discipleship by deepening the spiritual lives and religious commitment of their people. This goal has been the driving force behind my Ignatian program development work these last thirty years. I learned this focus from an experience I had while Director of Retreat Programs at Georgetown University. I discovered that the more intently we individually focus on developing our personal relationship with Jesus Christ, the more Christ draws us together as a community of believers—making us disciples of the Lord.

This revelation came in the most unexpected of ways. We conducted many different types of retreat programs through our office. Most were "talking" retreats with people sharing faith and working in group settings to discuss their hopes and dreams. One of our programs was a five-day silent Ignatian retreat. There were no faith-sharing sessions or group activities apart from Mass and Morning Prayer. Retreatants spoke to a spiritual director once-daily but even meals were in silence.

After several years' experience with both forms of retreat, I noticed that more lasting friendships and a deeper faith community were formed on the silent retreats. This puzzled me at first, but it soon became clear that the deep *personal encounter* with Christ that the retreatants experienced *in a communal setting* was the glue that formed such a lasting community. Christ was doing the work in our hearts by our opening to Him as Savior.

The final command of Christ in Matthew's Gospel is this: *Go, therefore, and make disciples of all nations, baptizing them in the name of the Father, and of the Son, and of the holy Spirit, teaching them to observe all that I have commanded you. And behold, I am with you always, until the end of the age"* (Mt 28: 19-20).

The goal of *Forty Weeks* is to draw all individuals in our Catholic faith communities into a daily personal encounter with Christ Jesus. I am convinced that the more we foster this daily personal relationship with Jesus, the more vibrant and joyful our faith communities will be. From this, we will indeed experience Christ present to us as we go forth and make disciples of all nations!

Leadership Requires Investing in Our Relationship with Jesus

As a pastor, RCIA director, faith formation leader, marriage prep counselor, campus minister, deacon or vocation director, you understand that the Christian life is, at its heart, a *relationship* with a person. That person is Jesus Christ. One must have their own relationship with Jesus in order to help others. There is a truth of the spiritual life that a teacher cannot take a student further than he or she has journeyed.

So I offer the thought that those of us who desire to lead others on a 40 week journey to Christ should first take the journey ourselves, or at least journey at the same time as those we seek to help. Strive to be a servant leading the way and supporting those you serve. St. Ignatius was a soldier before he was a saint. Ignatius knew that soldiers follow leaders who are the first one on the field and the last one off. Teach by this example.

Your experience as a leader for *Forty Weeks* will improve by reading (or using as reference) the book:

Sacred Story: An Ignatian Examen for the Third Millennium.
(further information available at:
[http://sacredstory.net/publications])

This book will give you the context for the *Examen* of St. Ignatius presented in *Forty Weeks*, and provide the background to help you understand your own journey to Christ. It will also help you answer others' questions in their experience of the *Forty Weeks* process.

Helping Others Invest in Sacred Story

In my many years of leading retreats, I encountered a paradoxical truth about *investment*. The programs were always more costly to run than retreatants could afford, and that required supplemental fundraising. Although the per-person cost was mostly subsidized, I always charged for the retreats. I learned that those who invested their money in the retreat were *far more likely* to invest energy in the experience of the retreat.

The *Forty Weeks* journey requires a significant personal investment of time, spirit and energy. It is no wonder that St. Ignatius used the word "exercises" to describe the prayer practices, meditations and contemplations. Engaging *Forty Weeks* is far more than reading a book - you will need to help those under your care to invest themselves in the journey as much as possible.

If you are a pastor, vocation director, faith formation leader, marriage prep counselor, RCIA coordinator or campus minister, **require** those interested in this prayer journey to first invest in the *Forty Weeks* book. We can offer the book at a considerable discount to your group, but I strongly suggest you ask individuals to buy the book with their own money, no matter whether you sell it to them at cost from your discount, or whether they buy the book directly. Those who *lay down money* for the book are more likely to *lay down their lives, pick up the cross and follow Christ* for the 40 weeks and hopefully, for the remainder of their days! Those who do not have financial resources to buy a book can still access the materials on our website [sacredstory.net] after registering for a free membership.

Christians from Other Denominations

During my doctoral project to shape the new *Sacred Story* Ignatian *Examen* method, I became convinced that Christian denominations other than Roman Catholics could also benefit from Ignatius' classic prayer discipline. My research therefore involved two groups: a large group of Roman Catholics and an equally sizeable group of Christians from a variety of Christian denominations. This group included Episcopalians, Lutherans, Baptists, Presbyterians, Evangelicals and those who described themselves as non-affiliated Bible Christians.

It was my experience that Ignatius' prayer method was as equally powerful and beneficial for the non-Catholic Christians as it was for the Roman Catholics. A key component of the *Forty Weeks* program is Sacramental Reconciliation. Some denominations offer Confession as a sacrament, others do not. Yet all benefited spiritually from writing out the Whole-Life Confession even if they did not formalize the Confession in a sacramental context.

I would encourage any Christian denomination who wants to use *Forty Weeks* to adapt the prayer methods to your unique context. Because God used Ignatius to develop a spirituality that fits seamlessly with the classic path of conversion, all serious Christians can benefit from Ignatian wisdom and tools, to deepen our relationship with Christ Jesus.

The Structure of the Book

The *Forty Weeks* book, you will note, has a contents page with section headings but does not identify page numbers for individual chapters. This is intentional. St. Ignatius urged spiritual directors to do everything possible to keep an individual focused on the present moment and the graces of that moment. He did not want people to jump around the materials. His *Spiritual Exercises*, and the prayer practices in *Forty Weeks*, are progressive and build on each other. The spiritual disciplines of *Forty Weeks* are designed to help an individual build a real, personal and heart-felt relationship with Jesus Christ.

As such, the book's format and structure works to keep individuals living in the present moment so this relationship has time to grow and develop. That is why we did not list each of the chapter titles and their page numbers. We want people to live the 40 weeks and let their relationship with Christ develop slowly. Encourage your participants to relax and take their time. They have their whole lives to grow close to Christ.

If you emphasize the "relational" dimension of the journey, this can temper the urge to skip around in the book. In fact, it is worth emphasizing that we will not gain the graces of the journey if we do that. One simply cannot fast-forward a relationship. A relationship with Christ takes time to develop—a lifetime in fact. Living that relationship *a day at a time* is the best way to deepen it. Do what you can in your leadership capacity to help participants to *live in the present moment* and focus on building a personal, heart-felt relationship with Jesus, the Divine Physician. There is no hurry.

Describing the Three Periods of *Forty Weeks*

Let me restate here some of Pope Francis' remarks on the most essential aspects of our Christian life. The first priority is Jesus Christ, and second, daily prayer to deepen my relationship with Jesus. Building on the first and second comes the third, witnessing my faith in Jesus in all my thoughts words and deeds.

If you are leading a group, you can explain that the prayer journey is divided into three periods that correspond closely with these three things:

✠   **THE FIRST PERIOD** is designed to help an individual pull together the narrative streams of one's life story. We are all used to compartmentalizing our experiences and most of us have never "seen," "felt" or "listened to" our life story holistically. This experience takes time. This first period is intended to help one to see, feel and listen holistically. One could even describe it as a sort of "archeological dig" into one's story and history.

This holistic digging and mapping expedition is geared toward helping us understand where we need healing so that each of us can bring our life to Jesus the Divine Physician, in a Whole-Life Confession. Jesus came to heal us and forgive us so we can bear fruit that endures to eternity. We really meet Jesus when we allow him to come to us in our weakness, sinfulness and need for transformation.

The confession takes place in Week 12 or 13 of this first period, depending on one's pace. I think it is very beneficial to mention to those embarking on the *Forty Weeks* journey that this Whole-Life Confession will come at the end of the first third of the 40 week journey. If people know they are moving toward something significant, they put more energy into the first leg of the journey. If people really invest themselves in excavating their life history in preparation for this Whole-Life Confession, they will have built a solid foundation for the second period and for their whole life

✠   **THE SECOND PERIOD** of the journey is learning the basics of the prayer method. Once I have met Jesus in the place where I most need healing, forgiveness and hope, it is essential to establish a daily ritual so I can continue to meet the Lord who grants those graces. Emphasize that *Sacred Story* prayer is a prayer "method" to help one open his/her heart to Christ Jesus in a deep, honest and meaningful *daily relationship*. This meeting began in the preparation for the Whole-Life Confession and in the confession itself.

You can best help those in your charge by reminding them that the goal of the second part of the journey is not to become a "master" or expert in a prayer discipline. The goal is to simply learn the rituals and structures of a new relationship well enough to find a daily "heart path" to Christ Jesus, the Divine Physician. All relationships need rituals and structure to help us maintain fidelity. Thus this second period can be likened to developing a new relationship. Establishing the rituals promotes fidelity to this relationship with Jesus that hopefully will last a lifetime.

✠ **THE THIRD PERIOD** of the journey engages participants in learning the language and structures of spiritual discernment so they can make the choices that give witness to Christ in daily life. At this point in the journey, all the discernment lessons are a necessary support to the daily practice (and all of the spiritual disciplines associated with the Ignatian *Examen* practice) in *Sacred Story* method. Spiritual discernment is an art that takes time to master.

Suggestions for Leading Groups through *Forty Weeks*

I.   WHAT TO EMPHASIZE

The most important thing to constantly emphasize for those journeying with *Forty Weeks* is that they are developing a personal relationship with Christ Jesus. Because of this, remind the individuals to focus less on *mechanics* and more on *relationship*. The mechanics of our prayer disciplines don't save us. They help us take the time to be present to the One who can save us: Jesus Christ. No one is judging our prayer performance in *Forty Weeks*.

Constantly remind your group to ask Jesus for help in opening their hearts and minds to God. Remind them to keep *asking for the graces* they need at the moment. Many people think that God is too preoccupied with *real problems* to have the time to be present to their concerns. In my experience, this attitude is terribly destructive to the supernatural life of grace that God desires for us. We need to overcome our timidity (or pride) and ask God *constantly* for the grace to daily come to Him with our sinfulness, weakness, hopes and dreams. Emphasize the relationship that the participants are developing with Jesus and remind them that it is a joint project between themselves and the Lord.

II.   USING THE **SACRED STORY** *FORTY WEEKS* DVD SERIES

The Sacred Story Institute ran a special program of *Forty Weeks* with over twenty parishes in the Archdiocese of Seattle. We followed a community of 35 adults, laity and pastors, over the course of the *Sacred Story* 40 week journey.

Included with the 9 DVDs is a set of discussion questions (found on a separate menu at the end of each disc). You can use these questions for faith-sharing groups at home or in your faith community to grow in your own relationship with Christ.

Disc One has two short explanatory videos (a 3 minute and a 9 minute version) that can be used for promotion/advertising. We encourage you to show the long or short Program Info videos to your faith or parish community. The Program Info videos provide a powerful testament to the program's dynamism and transformative powers. It will be a great way to encourage participation in this journey to Christ with *Sacred Story Prayer*.

The nine-disc series can be used however you desire. You can meet weekly and show 15 minutes each week as a discussion starter. You can meet periodically throughout the 40 week journey and watch one whole disc for a longer meeting/reflection.

We encourage those leading their group(s) to preview the different discs and determine how best to use them to help people move through this school of prayer and discernment.

The goal is not to be rigid in your use of the videos but allow them to be an aid to your journey. You will know best how to use them. The main thing to remember is that each individual's commitment to the daily disciplines is the MOST important thing you can emphasize for their benefit with the disciplines of *Sacred Story Prayer*.

Here is how the series is divided:

Disc One Weeks 1-4
Disc Two Weeks 5-8
Disc Three Weeks 9-13
Disc Four Weeks 14-16
Disc Five Weeks 17-19
Disc Six Weeks 20-27
Disc Seven Weeks 28-33
Disc Eight Weeks 34-37
Disc Nine Weeks 38-Eternity

Sacred Story Institute offers multiple ways for you to acquire the videos. Go to our website, [sacredstory.net] under the "PUBLICATIONS" tab at the top for the different ways you can acquire copies of this great aid to your Sacred Story 40 week journey to Christ.

III. WHEN TO MEET—FOSTERING DISCIPLESHIP

A weekly check-in of some nature is suggested, but the length and timing for weekly meetings will vary for different groups. As part of the process that led to this book, I met monthly with groups in all six parishes who were engaged in the 40 week journey. These meetings provided a wonderful opportunity for individuals to ask questions based on their prayer experiences and to find support in the experience of fellow participants.

With each group, something wonderful happened that was universal and deeply consoling. All six groups felt a great sadness when the regular meetings came to an end at the conclusion of the research project. They had grown so much in their faith and love of Christ, and had come to rely on the "community" experience of faith-sharing, such that they did not want it to end. You can expect this same dynamic to take place in your group.

Encountering Christ where we need His salvific love, and being with others who have encountered the Lord at this deep level, fosters the basic discipleship that has always renewed the Church in every age. So don't begrudge the time it takes for your meetings. Realize you are engaging people in a profound journey that will renew and reshape your community, university, parish or faith group.

If you have a large group, you might consider dividing into smaller faith-sharing groups who will meet weekly. If all these groups can meet at the same time in a central location with enough space, it will be more convenient for the overall group leaders. If this is not practical, small groups can meet weekly according to their own schedules. With this structure, the overall coordinator might suggest a monthly meeting with the entire group to answer the questions that have surfaced during the past month. Don't forget to consult the Encouragements & Wisdom supplements (available online) for insights along the journey.

An alternate arrangement is for small faith-sharing groups to send questions to the leader(s) based on issues that surface in the small groups and/or the weekly prayer journey. The leader(s) can respond to these questions via email prior to the small groups' next meeting.

IV. SOME SUGGESTIONS FOR VARIOUS PASTORAL CONTEXTS

✠   **PASTORS**: If you are a pastor leading a congregation through the journey, it is possible to take some time during the weekend Mass (at the beginning/end of the homily or in a comment at the beginning/end of Mass) to give a brief reflection for the past week and the coming week.

✠   **RCIA:** If you are an RCIA director, the *Forty Weeks* group meeting can be accomplished in the course of your regular meetings. The meeting could also be simply a discussion between the candidate and his/her sponsor. There are many opportunities in the context of RCIA for providential connections between *Forty Weeks* and the RCIA lessons leading up to Holy Week.

✠   **VOCATION DIRECTORS**: If you are a vocation director, you can offer the 40 week journey as part of a candidate's discernment process. The process of preparing for the Whole-Life Confession provides rich possibilities for helping a candidate deepen their conversion. It can also lead to a better understanding of how and why they want to serve the Church in priesthood or religious life. The candidate's spiritual director or the vocation director can provide further suggestions on how to bring the experiences of *Forty Weeks* to the discernment process.

✠   **FAITH FORMATION DIRECTORS**: Faith formation directors and deacons can profitably use *Forty Weeks* as part of a Bible Study, faith renewal program or individual spiritual direction. *Forty Weeks* can also be a great aid to laity in better engaging Sacramental Reconciliation, daily prayer and/or discernment.

✠   **CAMPUS MINISTERS**: If you are a campus minister for undergraduates and graduate students, *Forty Weeks* can be used in multiple ways: for RCIA programs; for year-long faith renewal programs; as a post-retreat program to deepen daily prayer life. If you work with faculty, staff and/or alumni, *Forty Weeks* can be useful in assisting busy adults to find a highly-focused, manageable set of daily prayer exercises that will aid them in a faith life that incorporates daily prayer, confession and discernment.

✠ **CLERGY FORMATION**: If you coordinate continuing formation for clergy, *Forty Weeks* can be used for a spirituality program in prayer formation. It can be used to support individual conversations with a spiritual director. It can also be used in conjunction with an annual retreat, using the book to set the themes of the annual retreat and then returning to *Forty Weeks* for a post-retreat renewal program. It can also be used to teach priests and deacons spiritual discernment in their own lives that can be powerfully applied to their ministries. *Forty Weeks* could also be a very valuable resource and basis for faith-sharing in Jesus Caritas groups.

 C3

THE MATERIALS

Listed below are the various elements of the *Sacred Story Examen* method presented in *Forty Weeks*. It is beneficial to understand these various components in your leadership role, so you can better navigate your way and lead others through the 40 week prayer journey.

The Meaning of Story in Forty Weeks Method

I use the title "STORY" in the *Forty Weeks* method because our lives are in fact a story linked to the great story of the universe. Jesus' life, death and resurrection is the "meta" STORY of the universe. Christians are called to participate in His SACRED STORY. By extension, narrative and parable are powerful means of evangelizing. *Sacred Story* points individuals to see their lives as a story linked to Christ's STORY that transcends time and space ("bearing fruit that endures to eternity," Jn 15:16). The *Examen* method of *Sacred Story* is focused on helping people find their way to the One "through whom and for whom everything was made" (Col 1:16); to become part of the greatest story ever told!

The Affirmations

Sacred Story Affirmations are a major tool in the *Forty Weeks* spiritual disciplines. The Affirmations distill much of the wisdom St. Ignatius presents in the "Rules for Discernment" in the first half of his *Spiritual Exercises*. The same Affirmations are repeated often and the Affirmations are found throughout the *Forty Weeks* book.

Frequently remind participants about the importance of saying these Affirmations aloud and paying attention to them throughout the whole journey. Make sure you yourself say them aloud. We "hear" much differently when we "affirm" something out loud, even if it is spoken softly. The Affirmations can even be used by a pastor as a homily conclusion, or by an RCIA director at the conclusion or start of a meeting. Basic sound advice such as, "I will not make any decision based on fear" is highly practical and valuable for the day-to-day spiritual journey. We strongly encourage you to learn the Affirmations and help others use them.

The Affirmations can be used productively in weekly meetings. As a way of fostering a spirit of discernment, invite individuals to notice which Affirmations occasion spiritual delight and which highlight spiritual frustrations. Invite *Forty Weeks* practitioners to ask themselves why they think the Affirmations inspire hope or discouragement. Have them ask God for the insight. These simple spiritual tools can provide profound breakthroughs in participants' spiritual journey by helping them better understand their history and sacred story. In this, they will be able to draw closer to Christ.

The Paradigm Charts and St. Ignatius' Progressive Conversion

There are four "paradigm charts" presented in the story of St. Ignatius (used in Weeks 2, 3, 4 of *Forty Weeks*). They are: The *Ignatian* Paradigm; The *Truth* Paradigm; The *Powerless* Paradigm and the *Patience* Paradigm. The first part of *Sacred Story: An Ignatian Examen for the Third Millennium,* gives a full description of St. Ignatius' spiritual awakening, explaining these model elements that frame his progressive conversion.

The "structures" of Ignatian spirituality emerge in the first awakening experience of St. Ignatius, described in *Sacred Story* as "the Ignatian Paradigm." Many saints, especially those who found religious communities, receive their distinct spirituality as a result of the founder's conversion process. Their pattern of sin and dysfunction becomes, by grace, a pathway to God for themselves and for others.

The success of the Society of Jesus' first several hundred years is due to our spirituality and the way it was used in early Jesuit ministries. Most of our pastoral work was engaging the laity in the use of the *Examen* in connection with frequent Confession (and Eucharist). An estimated 80-90% of our pastoral ministry was devoted to promoting these prayer disciplines from the first week of St. Ignatius' Spiritual Exercises. My goal in the *Forty Weeks Sacred Story* method is to use time-tested spirituality in support of the New Evangelization, which we have all been called to live as our part in spreading the Good News of Christ.

The Spiritual Diagnostic Charts

The spiritual diagnostics of the first section in *Forty Weeks* is designed to help individuals begin the "archeological mapping" process associated with their life-history—their *story*. It is worth continually reminding participants that all self-knowledge revealed via spiritual discernment falls along one of two trajectories. These patterns of "thoughts words and deeds" follow either the trajectory that moves us toward God or the trajectory that moves us away from God.

Encourage your group to keep revisiting their diagnostic charts and "reading" them in light of their own ongoing conversion process. As they move deeper into their prayer disciplines, they will "see" more in what they have written out initially, and they will discover more ideas for adding to those charts as they continue the process.

The MP3 Version of *Forty Weeks*

By the summer of 2015, the *Forty Weeks* book will be recorded in MP3 audio format as individual episodes for each weekly lesson. The episodes will ultimately cover the entire 40 week process. This way of digesting the material in the book can be helpful for many people, especially those who appreciate audiobooks via headphones or while driving. This free resource for your group will be available under the "Members" tab on [sacredstory.net], and you are welcome to share it!

The Web Version of *Forty Weeks*

The *Forty Weeks* method in its entirety is also available for free on the Sacred Story Institute website [sacredstory.net]. This is another way of digesting the materials. The web-based version includes layout and color pictures that were not possible to achieve in the printed versions or the eBook versions of *Forty Weeks*, and some may find the format more convenient.

The SACRED STORY *Forty Weeks* DVD Series

See above in "Getting Started" *USING THE SACRED STORY* FORTY WEEKS *DVD SERIES* for information on this powerful aid for your 40 week journey.

Finding Those Technology-Free Zones

The *Examen* has a powerful ability to help individuals hear the interior voice of conscience. All of us have experienced the daily erosion of contemplative moments where we might be able to recognize our conscience. Our world and our attention is now dominated by the technologies that demand our time and attention from the moment we rise in the morning until we lay down at night. (For further information on the impact of our tech-overload, I highly recommend Nicholas Carr's cautionary book *The Shallows*.[10])

We do our people a great service by challenging them to examine their technology use and helping them establish limits. We do this first by emphasizing the importance of those technology-free zones for the fifteen-minute *Sacred Story* prayer periods. Beyond that, we can help them examine their interaction with technology, and remind them to actively create room in their consciousness for awareness of spiritual influences (both the Divine Physician and human nature's enemy).

Encourage people to carve out sacred space during their daily and weekly schedules, to unhook from the technology grid and hook into the grid of nature, beauty and the spiritual world. During the week, encourage participants to experiment with turning off their phones and networks at 7 or 8 in the evening and going for a walk, exercising, reading a book or winding down with friends In real conversation. It is surprisingly restful to turn off the "data influx" and regain a measure of inner peace and quiet.

Suggest that people consider finding time on the weekends where they will turn off computers and cellphones. Perhaps Sunday can be a day to disconnect from the tech-network and reconnect with the "spiritual network." Many will be surprised at the difficulty of "switching off." Yet they will also discover how meaningful it is to open back up to the true sources of inspiration, renewal and human flourishing.

We need to discover most of all that true inspiration for our lives comes from the world of grace. We need to exercise our free-will, and discipline ourselves to turn our minds and hearts to God in all

---

[10] Nicholas Carr, *The Shallows: What the Internet is Doing to Our Brains*, (New York, W. W. Norton & Norton, 2010).

our thoughts, words and deeds. This will help us individually and as "a people set apart," to "produce fruit that will endure to eternity." (1 Pt 2:9, Jn 15:16)

‫ﮟ‬

ENCOURAGEMENTS AND WISDOM

Taking Full Advantage of the Resources

Let me provide some additional insights on the introductory materials in *Forty Weeks: An Ignatian Path to Christ with Sacred Story Prayer*.

How to Engage *Forty Weeks*

St. Ignatius became a great spiritual guide by surrendering his heart to Christ under the guidance of the Church. If Roman Catholics seek to follow the method and path of St. Ignatius, they must likewise develop a personal relationship with Christ and be docile to the Church's teaching and guidance as that relationship grows. Unity in the Body of Christ cannot be achieved if the individuals in the body each formulate his or her own rules of right and wrong. Ignatius' spiritual methods have clear boundaries and by following them, the legacy of sin in one's history can be transformed into a *Sacred Story*.

This is the fruit of following Ignatius' wisdom. All that is required to engage this spiritual journey is a generous heart and a willingness to be transformed by Christ's purifying forgiveness and mercy. It is the narrow path to holiness held out by the Church for millennia and the one followed by every saint in our history. The weekly lessons are challenging, but they are not complicated. Constantly invite individuals to pray for a generous heart and ask Christ for His help every step of the way.

The most common difficulty will be commitment to a daily, life-long personal relationship with Christ. To do so requires that one admit they need a Savior and call upon Him daily for help and guidance. This is, in effect, the daily action that reverses the Original Sin of separating from God. Help your people see the choice very starkly as committing to Christ daily and opening to their Sacred Story, or delaying the relationship and choosing to live a profane story. The choice really is that serious.

Additional Resources for Your Spiritual Journey

Constantly call attention to the other resources besides the core book to help your group along. The E&W (Encouragement and Wisdom) are very important aids for deepening participant understanding of the prayer materials. We count on leaders of all kinds to help us make *Forty Weeks* a better prayer resource. The book was a truly collaborative project between the Institute, the Holy Spirit and hundreds of lay faithful opening to God in their daily lives. We expect the resources to further develop each year under the Holy Spirit's guidance with the input of many wise souls.

In the Introduction to *Forty Weeks*, I strongly encourage feedback on the weekly lessons and the E&W. Please do so by signing up to be a Member at our website (go to [sacredstory.net]and click on the navigation link titled "**Members**.") Once you register, the "**Members**" section will be available to you. If you are facilitating a group through the *Forty Weeks* process, please indicate that in your feedback.

We also have a weekly "Advice" resource for your group (available on our website under the Members tab – look for the Supplemental Materials section with the title "Forty Weeks: Supplemental Leader Resources"). This "Advice" can serve as an additional help for your small group discussions and as

Pray ADVICE

encouragement to persevere in the journey. Note that the Advice begins on Week 3, because you will have MORE than enough to consider for Weeks 1 and 2 from the book alone!

It will be most helpful for you as leaders to review the Advice supplements about two weeks ahead of time, so you can be ready for the upcoming discussions. Here are the general themes that come up throughout the *Forty Weeks* Advice.

- Go slow! Everything about prayer points us back to patience, gratitude, and trust – going slow opens us to the Lord working through these.
- If we become anxious at any time during this prayer journey, we must pause and take a deep breath. Some of the reflections are challenging, but the Lord will bring us through it (see above!)
- Resist the impulse to become bored with repetition. As the slogan goes, "repetitio est mater studiorum" – repetition is the mother of learning! The more we internalize these lessons and prayers, the more the Spirit will use them to help us grow.
- Resist the impulse to become overwhelmed by new material. Some weeks present significant amounts of new information. We are not expected to process it all perfectly the first time through, and we can always review it later once we have additional practice.
- Anxieties and difficulties can be incredibly valuable if we surrender them to the Lord, asking that they be used as clues to the real source-wounds.
- Awareness of the present moment ("mindfulness") is key for us. As we go through the *Forty Weeks* journey, it will be an invaluable skill for us to hone, as it provides necessary information both on the Lord's actions in our lives and our own subconscious behavior.

Weekly Direct Communication with Participants (Send an Email)

We also suggest that you arrange a weekly communication with participants to keep them engaged. A simple email would suffice (perhaps including the weekly Advice text), or an announcement at Mass with a theme for participants to keep in mind for the particular week of this prayer journey. We have prepared just such emails in the Supplemental Materials (go to [sacredstory.net]; under the Members tab, look for the Supplemental Materials section with the title "Forty Weeks: Supplemental Leader Resources" -).

Share Your Experience with Us!

Tell us what helped you in your leadership role and what things you are finding beneficial in guiding others through the prayer materials. Tell us what you did not understand and propose suggestions to help clarify ideas or concepts. What you offer from your experience as a facilitator will greatly assist us in our ongoing commitment to refine these materials. Be Not Afraid!

‎ಛ

II

WHOLE-LIFE CONFESSION
&
FAITH-SHARING GROUPS

THE WHOLE-LIFE CONFESSION

Details for Hosting a Whole-Life Reconciliation Service

Here are some elements to consider when hosting a Whole-Life Reconciliation service at your parish or center.

Ratio of Priests to People —When we offered our services in the Archdiocese of Seattle, we held individual services in each of the six parishes participating in the research/ beta project. Every pastor participated in his own service and many of these pastors also participated in the services at the other parishes. It is recommended to limit the service to two hours.

To accomplish this, we sought to have one priest for every ten persons who would be present to make a Whole-Life Confession. Since the program instructs participants to write out their confession and to limit the written confession to 1000 words or less, it takes about 10-15 minutes per person for each individual confession. Therefore, plan on having one priest for every 10-12 penitents if you run a two hour service. If you lengthen the service, you can double the number of penitents per priest.

Face to Face & Anonymous—It is best that each of the priests be available for confession *both* face-to-face *and* anonymously. This can be achieved by setting a prie dieu behind the priest's chair and also setting a chair in front of the priest. If there are not a sufficient number of prie dieus, a chair or a simple kneeler could be set up behind the priest. Some parishes may have

Reconciliation Rooms that can accomplish this dual method, but it is best to make the option available (if possible) for *each* priest to hear confessions face-to-face or anonymously.

Privacy—St. Ignatius urged those praying during a retreat to go to a private place where they would have the freedom to engage in prayer without worrying about others. Confessions will be written out and read by the penitents. It is vital that those making a confession feel comfortable enough to clearly read their letters aloud and to express emotions should they be so moved. Although it may not be possible to have enclosed rooms for each priest, it is important to strive for audio and visual isolation for the priests and penitents.

Order of the Service—It is best to keep the service and opening remarks simple and brief. Focus instead on the one-on-one confession time. Because individuals have been preparing for this confession for 12 weeks, a lengthy introduction and/or examination of conscience is not necessary.

Here is a possible template for a simple Service of the Word ahead of the individual confessions:

✠ Give some short introductory remarks to explain the service.

✠ Offer an Opening Prayer.

✠ Read Gospel Passage Jn 20: 20-30.

✠ Offer a very simple word of encouragement and then explain the mechanics of the service. Encourage people to "be not afraid."

✠ Have your bishop write a short letter of encouragement, to be read after the Gospel passage. We have included at the end of this section the letter Archbishop Sartain (Archdiocese of Seattle) wrote for our six beta-project parish services. If multiple parishes are doing the *Forty Weeks* program, the local ordinary can write a unique letter that is addressed to each individual parish, or write a general letter for all parishes.

✠ Purchase a very simple small wood crucifix or cross for each penitent or order the Sacred Story Cross. For our beta-project, I bought small olive wood rosary-kit crucifixes (made in the Holy Land; they were about $0.50 each ordered in bulk via a rosary supply company).

The Sacred Story Cross can also be useful, as it reminds people of both the Ten Commandments and the five movements of *Sacred Story Prayer*: Creation, Presence, Memory, Mercy and Eternity (for ordering details, see our website [sacredstory.net], under the PUBLICATIONS tab; available beginning Spring 2015).

Put all the crucifixes on a small table at the head of the sanctuary. Have the crucifixes blessed and ask each participant to take one before going to confession. It is amazing how such a simple symbol takes on so much meaning. Remember, participants have been preparing for this confession for three months. Many of the 180 people who made a Whole-Life Confession in our research beta-project have carried those crosses with them since that service.

✠ Encourage participants to stay until everyone has gone to confession. Ask that, if their schedules allow, they pray for themselves and for those attending this service and all other Whole-Life Confessions that may be taking place in other parishes.

✠ Use either recorded or live music during the service. It should be gentle and reflective. If you have musicians who can provide this ministry, this is preferable.

Transcending Difficulties That May Arise

As participants approach the experience of the Whole-Life Confession, there are a number of issues that need to be addressed. Here are some of the most important challenges and possible solutions:

✠ *Someone missed the parish Whole-Life Confession service.*

Have them arrange an alternate service with a parish/priest willing to help. Or more simply, you can find a priest who will hear your Whole-Life Confession. **The priest need not be familiar with** ***Forty Weeks* for this to be a positive experience!**

This appointment will consist of them reading their letter to Jesus (no more than 20 minutes) and receiving sacramental absolution. Remember the instructions from Week 12. Simply explain to the priest that you are going through a prayer-renewal program oriented around the spiritual exercises of St. Ignatius, and that the first twelve weeks of prayer have focused on opening your life-history to the healing of Jesus the Divine Physician.

✠ *What if an individual does not want to go to their parish priest for their Whole-Life Confession?*[11]

---

[11] Fr. Watson makes a 4-hour trip each direction every month to see his confessor/spiritual director. This is an important event! Think of it as a pilgrimage, and seek out a priest for this occasion. Yes, priests are busy but you would be surprised how many priests are renewed by hearing a heartfelt confession. You are not only arranging a unique Whole-Life Confession, you are also laying the foundation for a habit of monthly confession (and possibly finding a good confessor for life who can help you grow in your relationship with Christ). The Holy Spirit will assist you to make a commitment for monthly Confession with a regular confessor. Remember:

Ask and it will be given to you; seek and you will find; knock and the door will be opened to you. For everyone who asks, receives; and the one who seeks, finds; and to the one who knocks, the door will be opened. Which one of you would hand his son a stone when he asks for a loaf of bread, or a snake when he asks for a fish? If you then, who are

This is why it is helpful to bring in other priests for the service at your parish. Remember, individuals should also be able to receive the Sacrament anonymously so make sure to set up your service where this is possible.

So, be not afraid to ASK the Spirit for help!

✠ *What if it is not possible for me to finish my Whole-Life Confession letter?*

Take the time you need to get it done, keep going, and eventually you will finish it. Remember you are not climbing Mt. Everest; just writing a letter to Jesus.

✠ *What if it is not possible for me to make a sacramental Whole-Life Confession?*

- First, it will always be possible to make a Whole-Life Confession. It may take a bit more time and effort, but you will be able to do this. In the time before the actual event, remember that the exercise of writing the letter to Jesus is your preparation. The Lord—the Divine Physician—will lead you to the priest who can assist with the sacrament of Reconciliation.
- Second, if you are not able to complete the experience by bringing it to sacramental reconciliation until later after Week 13, do not despair! Keep moving forward with the lessons of *Forty Weeks*. You will be amazed at how the work of Weeks 1-13 will continue to bear fruit in the later lessons!
- Finally, it is worth remembering that in Fr. Watson's

---

wicked, know how to give good gifts to your children, how much more will your heavenly Father give good things to those who ask him. (Mt 7: 7-11) doctoral research which helped form *Forty Weeks*, a number of non-Catholic Christians participated in this "Whole-Life Confession" exercise. Because they could not have the sacramental experience, many of them simply read the letter to a friend or fellow participant. This may be an alternative for you until you are able to receive sacramental absolution when the Lord does bring the priest into your life.

A Few Things to Remember Overall

✠ Encourage participants to take personal responsibility for their own spiritual growth! Don't let action or inaction be dictated by what may or may not be happening in one's faith community. The Whole-Life Confession is an important moment and a major opportunity to take ownership of one's spiritual life. It may take some work to arrange an experience of sacramental Whole-Life Confession – do not let that deter you! We always stretch ourselves for things in our lives that are important. Nothing is more valuable or more important than our relationship with Christ, the Divine Physician, who seeks to heal us so that our lives bear fruit that endures to eternity.

✠ Finally, realize that no experience is ever "perfect" and no priest or confession experience is perfect either. As with all things in our lives, the Lord takes what is imperfect and makes it perfect *eventually,* using the imperfect for our growth in His love. So be open to the action of the Spirit, even in the less-than-perfect circumstances of life!

Comments from Priests who Participated in the Whole-Life Confession

✠ "The confessions evince that the program touches the exercitants. The idea of writing a letter to Jesus Christ frees these people to speak their inmost thoughts and feelings. I have been

moved by the depth of these confessions. They are heart-felt. A notable aspect is that the letters tend to reflect multi-year feelings and thoughts. This ensures that trivia are left behind; long-standing shadows congregate and receive focus. In all of these meetings, holiness comes forward."
- *Fr. Emmett Carroll, SJ (St. Cecilia Church, Bainbridge Island)*

✠ "I was touched and encouraged by the whole-life confessions in the Sacred Story project. Truly the in-depth preparation and unique formula for the confession proved to be a source of special graces of wisdom and conversion for the participants."
-*Fr. Bob Egan, SJ (Seattle University)*

✠ "I was greatly moved by hearing the confessions of persons in the Sacred Story spiritual program. They had prepared for the sacramental encounter with deep reflection and awareness of God's compassion and their need for it, and expressed themselves and their sorrow from the depths of their being. I felt privileged to give them the forgiveness of God and of the church."
-*Fr. David Leigh, SJ (Seattle University)*

✠ "The Sacred Story program addresses a very serious need in adult faith formation. Many Catholics have lost touch with any sort of felt-need for the kind of transformation and healing that can come through the Sacrament of Reconciliation. As a result, long-festering inner woundedness, guilt, and shame can drag the faithful into a persistent spiritual malaise, a genuine desolation. In some, perhaps most cases, the existence of this malaise as well as its deeper causes never come to awareness. Moreover, feelings of guilt and shame and the fear of judgment can, in a powerful but often unacknowledged way, hold the faithful back from reaching out for the healing offered in the Sacrament. As I observed when participating in the whole-life confession part of the Sacred Story program, Sacred Story guides participants very gently through a process of self-examination. It helps them to reexamine the ragged edges of sin in their lives—their own personal sin and the sin of others that has wounded them—and to relocate those dimensions of their experience in the larger story of God's love for them, the love revealed in Jesus, but also the love that has accompanied them all along the way, even in their times of darkness. The power and grace of this experience was evident to me in the expressions of release and relief on the faces of those who shared their stories with me. "

-Fr. Jim Voiss, SJ (Rector, Jesuit Community Gonzaga University)

✠ "I am very grateful for the opportunity to have heard Sacred Story whole life confessions. It was evident that all of the participants dedicated much prayer and thought to prepare for the sacrament and it was a privilege for me to hear them. I was especially struck by the depth of sharing which recalled the sort of intimacy usually only possible as part of a lengthy retreat. In the end, I feel I was blessed to receive much more than I gave and would welcome the opportunity to participate in the Sacred Story project again."

-Fr. Eric Watson, SJ (Seattle University)

✠ "What made a deep impression on me with most of them was their ability to place their lives within a context—what I would call a context of grace—so that they were not simply confessing a list of sins that only reveals the symptoms. Also, I noticed how many expressed gratitude to God for what they have received and what they now have; even grateful for the sins and shortcomings which brought them to this moment of conversion, and the awareness of their need for God."

-Fr. Tim Clark (Our Lady of the Lake Church, Seattle)

✠ "It was a profoundly moving experience for me as a priest to receive the whole life confessions of those who participated in the Sacred Story program. It was a very sacred experience to be the recipient of life stories that went deep into the heart of the penitents. Many wept with both sorrow and joy as they opened their lives to the healing power of Jesus and for the first time let

his forgiveness and love flow deep into their wounded past. Many came to the exercise with a certain amount of fear and trepidation but walked out with a new freedom—the freedom of a loved and forgiven child of God".
-*Fr. John Madigan (Holy Rosary Church, Seattle)*

✠ "Hearing these full life confessions was a unique experience for a priest. Often in the confessional we priests hear hurried confessions or confessions that seem routine. The wonderful thing about these confessions was that they were all the fruit of much thought and prayer. These penitents wanted to be there—even if they were frightened by the depth of the experience. Here people were putting the pieces of their lives together by God's grace, and were in the midst of a prayerful process that would help them heal from what their memories and prayers had revealed. I would recommend this way of celebrating the sacrament of reconciliation to all priests."
-*Fr. Kurt Nagel (Holy Family Church, Kirkland)*

✠ "I thought the Confessions were good and thoughtful. I had many of the penitents tell me that it was a very helpful and freeing process. It was especially helpful for them to see the trends that were traced throughout their lives and recognize how that sin has touched and warped many aspects of their lives. Many found it an emotional and deeply moving experience."
-*Fr. Hans M. Olson (St. Mary Magdalene Church, Everett)*

☞

Dear Sacred Story Participants,

In these final weeks of the Easter Season, we become even more conscious that the ministry of the Lord Jesus is one of reconciliation -- for us individually, for our Church, and for every human person made in the image of God. We know that he came that "we might have life and have it to the fullest." We also know that he came to create the "new heavens and a new earth" through his triumph over sin, sickness, and even death itself.

What you have been doing these past 12 weeks with your Sacred Story prayer journey is opening your hearts and minds to the most profound truths of our Faith, which are also the true story of love and hope offered to all people of this and every age. My sincere congratulations for your efforts to both open yourselves

to Christ and to offer your experiences to the Sacred Story Institute for the benefit of thousands of other Catholics.

Please know that in the time of your whole-life confession, each of you will have a special place in my prayers and Masses. May you encounter the Christ who told the disciples in the upper room, "Peace be with you." This is our brother, Lord, and Savior, Jesus, who, in giving the gift of the Holy Spirit to the newborn Church, commanded his disciples to forgive sins.

You are sharing in the very center of the Christian message by offering your entire lives to the Lord for his healing, forgiveness and enlightenment. It is my sincere prayer that you experience the abundant grace of his forgiving love. May that love propel you forward in your sacred story journey so that you may bear fruit that endures to eternity. With every best wish and prayer, I am

Sincerely in Christ,

Most Rev. J. Peter Sartain
Archbishop of Seattle

FAITH-SHARING GROUPS GUIDELINES

For Use with all Forms of Faith/Prayer Discussion Groups[12]

The following guidelines are offered to help leaders better facilitate prayer groups; men's or women's support groups; Bible study groups, and similar small-group gatherings.

Structure and Purpose of Small Groups:

Faith-sharing groups provide an occasion for members to share and learn from others in dealing with real-life issues. These groups provide sacred space to listen to others' experience and to speak one's own heart and mind. The opportunity may arise, if time permits, for members to engage each other in discussion and questions. However, the primary purpose is to listen - to one's own heart and to the hearts of others.

The format we have found most fruitful for these groups is based loosely on a Quaker-style meeting. In these, reverence for the individual is primary. Everyone sits together in gentle silence until someone feels inspired to speak. The person so inspired speaks while others listen. There is no rebuttal or response. The statement stands as an expression of that person's faith and experience. Until someone else feels moved to speak, the group

---

[12] These guidelines are adapted from my thirty years of retreat work and can benefit almost any faith-reflection group format.

will sit in silence once more. It is a different way of paying attention to what someone has to say. Often, when someone speaks, we stop listening and begin formulating our response to them before they have even stopped speaking. With the option of immediate response removed, we are afforded the opportunity to simply listen—to God, others and our own hearts.

Leaders are present in the groups to participate fully in the listening as well as to offer their own reflections. They are also there to facilitate the process so that everyone has the chance to speak. Because this format may not be familiar to everyone, here are some guidelines to help the process go smoothly:

Getting Settled

GIVE AN OVERVIEW:

Upon starting a new group, people will most likely be a little nervous. To ease the tension, take a short period of time to settle. Ask everyone to get comfortable. Allow a few minutes and then explain that the time together will fall into three parts (listening, comment, and prayer). Explain what each of these parts entail and the expected time-frame. With groups of 5-8 people, it takes at least 40 minutes to engage all three parts of the process.

SET YOUR TIME:

We strongly suggest limiting your gathering to no more than one hour. Whatever amount of time you choose, reassure the group that you are tracking the time so they do not need to be concerned. At the start of each gathering, take three to five minutes for silent reflection on the theme you will be discussing today. It is best if the overall program coordinator can restate the focus of reflection/sharing, to ensure that it is clear to everyone in the group. This will save time and improve the group process for everyone.

Before any one speaks, we recommend taking about three to five minutes of quiet time for participants to listen to their hearts in light of the theme. Silence is a very powerful prayer medium. The leader should explain this process clearly and manage the time for the group, announcing when the three to five minutes have ended.

CONFIDENTIALITY:

Make it clear from the start that what is said in the small group is sacred and is not to be shared outside the group. Ask the members of the group to agree to keep confidential what is shared in the group. This needs to be a solemn pledge. As a leader, it is important to set an environment of trust and confidentiality. Let people know that this time is for them to say what they think and feel, without worrying about judgment or being discussed with a third party. This is a private time just for this group.

SPEAK OUT OF THE "I":

Invite those sharing to speak out of their own experience. Instead of projecting feelings and thoughts to the general "you" as in "you know when you feel like..," encourage people to own their feelings and thoughts. You may remind the individuals in the group to say: "I believe; I think; I feel," etc. It can take one or two small groups before people catch on to this speaking out of the personal "I".

ANXIETY:

It is natural for there to be some initial anxiety in the group. People may not know each other or may be nervous because they do not know what to expect. I have two suggestions to ease this tension. First, be open and honest about how you are feeling. This tends to quickly put people at ease. You might mention that you are nervous because you have never facilitated a group like this before. Second, let people know the full small group structure. This helps remove the fear of the unknown. I recommend inviting their cooperation by asking; "does that sound that okay?" after explaining what is to happen next. Asking for input and participation helps individuals accept ownership of the group experience.

Part One: Reflections/Listening

ONE AT A TIME:

After initial five minutes of silent reflection conclude, explain that the first part of the time is for everyone to share his or her reflections on the particular theme. Mention that there is no particular order to follow and that everyone should speak when they feel comfortable.

✠ People should speak one at a time
✠ People should not interrupt each other
✠ Ask that each individual say when he or she is finished

To ensure everyone has a chance to speak if they wish, no one person should speak for longer than four or five minutes. If there is time remaining at the end, there can be a second go around with perhaps a two minute per-person guideline.

ALLOWING REFLECTIONS TO STAND ALONE:

During this first part, people should not comment on or offer advice in response to others. The experience of being listened to without comment or judgment is often a rare gift. In this group situation, a space is created where the primary purpose is to listen to each other.

BE COMFORTABLE WITH SILENCE:

Everyone should be invited to speak his or her own mind and conscience. However, no one in the group should feel obligated or forced to speak. There will inevitably be some awkward silences because this type of gathering is different from everyday conversation. Do not let it bother you. It is normal. Ask people to say "pass" or a similar phrase to indicate that they do not wish to speak. Leaders must never be afraid of silence in a group. It is much better to be silent together while waiting for someone to speak than it is to fill up the silence with chatter. There is nothing wrong with silence. Leaders need never feel as though they are doing something wrong if people are not speaking.

SOME CHOOSE TO LISTEN AND NOT SPEAK:

There is a possibility that some will choose not to talk. There could be many reasons for this. Be sensitive to those who may want to speak but may be shy initially. Others may not have the capacity to quickly articulate their thoughts or experiences. The introverts in the group might need more time to get to the point of speaking. The extroverts might need to take less time speaking to allow this. You will find the right balance.

EMOTIONAL INTENSITY:

If someone shares a reflection that is particularly thoughtful or emotional, allow some additional time for that reflection to be absorbed. Remember that a powerful reflection can make some participants feel that they don't have anything important to contribute (similar to the dynamic when someone says something brilliant and ends the discussion for everyone). People are at different points in their lives and need to know that they have the freedom in this group to be exactly where they are. The most important thing to keep in mind is to ask if everyone who wanted to speak had the opportunity to do so before concluding part two.

Part Two: Comment

When everyone has been given the opportunity to say something, open discussion and comments can take place. If so inclined, the group leader can make some personal observations about what the members of the group shared and can also say what he or she experienced in listening to others. People should be invited to offer comments and observations on the reflections and experiences that they just heard. Some might also want to augment their own reflections at this time.

People can also ask questions. This is the least important part of the group, however, because this type of conversation can happen easily outside the group. If there is a great deal of time left after the Reflections/Listening, it may be a good idea to take another five minutes of silence and return for another round of Reflections/Listening.

Part Three: Closing Prayer

The leader should be aware of the time and note when five minutes are remaining. At this point, it is time to conclude. Everyone may not have had the opportunity to speak, but remind the group that there will be other times to continue this discussion. It is also worth reminding the group that there is never enough time to get extremely in-depth during the faith-sharing groups, and that is not really their purpose.

To end, the leader can propose taking a few moments of silence, followed by an invitation to voice prayers or petitions, before closing with the Our Father or another prayer. Ask the group if they approve of this conclusion. If not, solicit suggestions and try to accommodate the group. It may be best if a different group member volunteers to lead the closing prayer each time the group meets. If you can find a simple ritual that everyone agrees on, the group will join in more readily.

GUIDELINES AND HELPFUL HINTS:

1) Share any difficulties

Leaders ought to discuss group difficulties with an adult faith formation director and/or other leaders. The director and other leaders will be able to give guidance, or on the rare occasion that it becomes necessary, speak to someone in the group who may be having difficulty.

2) Create an atmosphere of trust

It is vital to create an atmosphere of trust within the group so participants feel free to discuss their lives in the context of their faith. Leaders should remember their responsibility to support this environment. Because faith is the reason we share, trust that God will be present with grace to see them and the group through. Leaders do not need to make this explicit. It is enough to keep it in their minds and hearts.

3) Pray for courage and wisdom to focus on real issues

It is difficult for people to discuss personal thoughts and reactions on the level of faith. It Is easy to become distracted by peripheral issues. Leaders serve the group best by guiding the discussion to a deeper level of personal lived experiences, faith, and belief. This is why honesty on the part of leaders is essential. They need to help the individuals in the group to move into this territory by setting an example. This kind of leadership takes faith, conviction, and courage. Leaders should ask God to help them provide a context for people to experience His love and fidelity in the time spent together. The Lord always honors such requests.

4)   Be realistic about how much can be accomplished

Leaders should remember that the times together for small group sharing will necessarily only "scratch the surface." It is impossible to fully explore a conversation in these groups. Leaders must realize that this group experience is only a beginning. Issues cannot be completely wrapped up and packaged in less than an hour (this is normal!). If participants desire this level of conversation, they will need to make some choices in how they live their "regular" lives.

5)   Don't be afraid to lead

By virtue of familiarity with the materials, leaders have authority in the eyes of their group, even though some participants may be older than the leaders. People will look to leaders for some guidance. Leaders may be tempted to blend in with the group as peers among peers, but they also have to guide the conversation. Leaders need not be afraid of this leadership role! Others will expect it.

6)   Honesty is more important than knowing it all

Leaders may become anxious when they think they need to be perfect or instant experts on all topics. Instead, they will do better to know why a topic is part of the prayer journey and review their own reactions to the topic with their group. Leaders need to share some of their head as well as their heart. They should lead with honesty and openness.

7)   Invite, never force

Leaders facilitate to ensure that everyone who so desires has a chance to speak. Leaders will discover that some people are not speaking. This may be because they are shy and need encouragement, or because they do not have anything to say at the moment and are content to listen to others. Never force people to speak. Invite and be content with what individuals choose to share or not share.

8) Be patient with yourself and others

Leaders should realize that leading a group can be a challenge, and therefore should not demand too much of themselves. The sensitivity and finesse needed is gained by practice. This can be an important learning experience.

TROUBLESHOOTING

The following are some anxieties and problems that may arise in faith-sharing groups, along with some helpful suggestions on how to address them:

a. The Leader need not have all the answers:

Remember, the leader is merely a facilitator for discussion, not a spiritual expert. Most questions that arise in small groups are lifelong questions and cannot be solved by a simple response from the leader. The most important part of the small group is providing the room for people to reflect on significant life and faith issues, rather than having all the answers to those questions.

b. A member of the group is talking too much:

It is important for the leader to facilitate discussion for all. In this case, simply ask the person to remember the 4-5 minute rule so that everyone has time to talk.

c. Some dramatic news is dropped by a group member:

There is nothing wrong with serious and sometimes dramatic news being shared in a confidential small group setting.

Sometimes when this happens however, a single person's issues can become the entire focus of one or more small group sessions, thus preventing others from sharing their own concerns.

Keep focused on the fact the not all of life's complications can be solved in a single gathering. Hold sacred the important experience that has been shared but work to make room for others to have their time as well. Let individuals know that sometimes it is beneficial to seek counseling for issues that may be difficult to fully share in a group setting. It is possible that a buried wound can surface with an emotional, spiritual, and psychological intensity that is best handled by a more experienced person and in a more personal one-on-one setting.

d. Someone appears completely uninvolved in the group:

Leaders need to understand that many different personalities are present in a small group. Just because someone is choosing not to speak or seems aloof, does not mean that he/she is not getting something out of the group (in fact they may be inwardly very engaged!). Alternately, if someone's aloofness is aggressive or in some way disruptive to the others, the leader can privately ask the individual if he or she is having some difficulty. This will usually surface any real problems and provide a solution for the rest of the meetings. If not, in confidence politely point out any behaviors which may be causing problems for others, and ask the person if they would be mindful of this for the sake of the others in the group.

CB

III

THEOLOGICAL
BACKGROUND

THE SACRED STORY PRAYER METHOD

The Five-Part Meditation

The five-part meditation forms the heart of the *Sacred Story's Examen* prayer method: Creation, Presence Memory, Mercy and Eternity. The book, *Sacred Story: An Ignatian Examen for the Third Millennium*, offers a full explanation of how the classic Ignatian *Examen* has been incorporated into this new framework. These Five Meditations encapsulate the "conversion paradigm" of the *Spiritual Exercises.* It is this paradigm that has made the *Spiritual Exercises* so durable over the years.

The challenge in making the classic Ignatian *Examen* more accessible was to remain faithful to Ignatius' structure, purpose and desired outcomes but make the five movements more intelligible to today's Catholic. Our research with hundreds of volunteers has been very encouraging. Prayed faithfully, life-transformative changes are not uncommon.

The pedagogy in *Forty Weeks* is designed to give practitioners as much time as they need to learn the themes of the meditations so they are able to internalize them and "know them by heart." I constantly hear people worry about "doing it right." I always emphasize "relationship." In your role as a group leader, constantly remind your participants that the five movements open us to God's grace *by the relationship* with God that they help facilitate. It is the relationship that is important, not a mechanistic recitation or a "perfect" performance on an individual's part.

If you were meeting the Queen of England, you would have to follow a set protocol of bowing, not turning your back on her and using the right words to address her. You would be worried in this instance if you were "doing it right." But with the Lord, the *prayer structure facilitates your relationship*. It does not define the substance of the relationship. Learn the difference and help others learn it too.

If you had a regularly scheduled meeting with an individual and you always covered five specific areas of your relationship with that person, all your meetings would not be the same. Some meetings you might address one or two of the themes and spend most of your time with those topics, only briefly mentioning the others. The next meeting might forgo the previous themes covered in-depth and focus on one or more of the others that were only briefly discussed previously. This is true of the Five Meditations in the fifteen-minutes set periods of prayer.

This attention to the most significant themes in each meeting speaks to the "relational" character of the prayer and is the natural way relationships actually play out. If you were approaching the prayer mechanistically, you would always use the exact same amount of time for each part of the meditation, *and never vary*. But heartfelt relationships don't work this way.

Relationships grow by addressing what is most significant each time you visit with the person. In this case, the person we are approaching is the Lord and we come to him with our whole life.

But because we want to keep the *whole relationship* before our minds and hearts, we recite the Five Meditations at the beginning and at the end of the fifteen-minute prayer session. By bookending our prayer this way, we are constantly "awakening" to our lives from creation to eternity. Our bookend recitation also helps us to gradually "awaken" to the present moment, linking it to our memories so we can better understand the mercy we need to offer and receive.

It is essential to keep the five word bookends as part of each set prayer period. Some days I may primarily rejoice and give thanks for the gifts of CREATION. Another day I may be suffering and primarily struggling with MERCY. In the first instance, I must remind myself that all gifts of CREATION are sustained by God's Mercy. In the second, I need to remember that even though I am suffering at present, God is a loving and creating God who will remain faithful to me and to the Church until "the end of the age." All five meditations, intentionally remembered, help shape my mind and heart.

These Five Meditations entail the entire mystery of Creation, the Fall, and our Redemption in Christ. They never wear out! By our fidelity to this relationship in Creation, Presence, Memory, Mercy and Eternity, we deepen our awareness of the God who created us, sustains us with love and forgiveness and seeks to draw us into an eternal Kingdom.

The Prayers on Waking and Upon Retiring

I can't emphasize enough how significant these two prayer moments are if practiced daily. Constantly ask your group if they are doing them, and if they say no, tell them to get to work. Think of them as short "stretching" exercises. If engaged regularly, they help all our other "spiritual exercises" throughout the days and months to produce more fruit.

The *intentional* turning to God on waking and before retiring (with the content of my heart- peaceful or agitated), works powerfully against the *darkness of sin* that renders us unconscious of God and of the state of our souls. We have to consciously and regularly awaken to the spiritual world or we lose sight of it and our true nature.

By doing this short, powerful awareness prayer twice daily, we can help people *begin* to see their lives as supremely important to the Loving Creator who desires to receive both our gratitude and our sufferings in each and every moment. We become aware of our hopes, joys and fears, and we become aware of the only One who can help us. Emphasize this simple short discipline and do it yourself! By doing it yourself, you will understand its great merit!

Exercises during the Day

These exercises are St. Ignatius' *General Examen* and *Particular Examen* components. Remember, the *General Examen* identifies sins and dysfunction of our corporeal or bodily nature. These are the unique destructive, addictive, compulsive and sinful habits that we use as narcotic for life's difficulties and pains. The *Particular Examen* identifies sins and dysfunction of our spiritual nature. It is the particular way pride/narcissism manifests in our history, passively or aggressively. It is our root sin that displaces God in favor of the *self* as god.

It is humanly impossible for any individual to comprehend all of one's sins in thoughts, words and deeds. But our prayer calls each of us to awaken to where and why we each need Jesus as Savior. Knowing what is sinful is the first step. At the *General Examen* level of spiritual awareness, we acknowledge what is sinful (based on the Scriptures, Commandments and Tradition) and *honestly name it* as it manifests in our history. When we have honestly assessed our history and seen our *tendencies*, we then begin to notice in the course of the day when we are tempted and when we give in to temptation.

The same is true of understanding the root sin of pride. We must identify how our narcissism displaces God, elevating our *self* as god. When we have honestly identified that we are narcissists who seek, passively or aggressively, to elevate ourselves over others and God, we can begin to notice *when* it happens in the course of our day.

For both the *General* and *Particular Examen*, we want to do the full *awareness exercises* for only the most striking examples of each pattern. The goal is to *become conscious* of when and how we are tempted and fail. We limit ourselves to doing the *General* and *Particular* awareness exercises only 2-3 times a day so that we don't fall into the trap of obsessiveness that nearly derailed St. Ignatius' conversion. By stopping 2-3 times a day for the most notable events on the *General* and *Particular* level, we will gradually awaken to more and more of the events as they manifest in the course of our waking hours. The awakening is gradual and comes in God's time, not our own.

The principal thing to emphasize with yourself and others is only doing 2-3 full awareness exercises per day. The discipline of limiting oneself to 2-3 times for the full exercises is essential for it to become a sustainable life-long spiritual activity.

The Daily, Weekly & Monthly Journal Exercises

Individuals will succeed in their commitment to the journal exercises if they focus clearly on two elements. First, they must know what they are documenting with the journal exercise. They are writing down the principal spiritual movements from the day—the principal inspiration and the principal counter-inspiration. They are noting *when these movements happen* and *to what they are attached*.

Real things inspire and real things counter-inspire. What was the "thing" and what spiritual signature did it have? This additional awareness exercise attunes us to the spiritual world and opens us to the need for spiritual discernment.

Second, they are only to write two sentences or two phrases.

They are to document the principal spiritual inspiration and the principal counter-inspiration. This should take only a minute or two! If participants try to write more extensively, the exercise will not be sustainable. The writing must be simple, short, and to the point. This is not a diary or a memoir.

The daily, weekly, and monthly sifting of these two simple statements will have a profound impact on awakening the practitioner to how she/he is tempted and how both God's grace and evil's deceptions play out in daily life. AND, it is unbelievably valuable material for the monthly Confession.

The Practice of Sacramental Reconciliation

People should commit to monthly Reconciliation with the same priest each month. We all need the accountability and the grace the Sacrament affords. We also need the same spiritual doctor helping us month to month if we desire that the Sacrament also be a forum for spiritual direction. Of course our sins are still forgiven if we seek a new priest each month. But different priests each month never see the whole story.

We don't go to a new doctor each time we seek advice for the same chronic medical condition. We should consider this "spiritual therapy" in a similar way. As a leader, you will need to overcome complaints about how difficult it is to find a priest "they like." If we had cancer, we would find the best doctor we could, and go to great lengths to do also! This is even more important, though it may not seem so initially! If individuals ask God for help and give Confession the priority in life it deserves, a good priest will, by God's grace, become available. And if individuals take the time to prepare for the Sacrament by daily prayer, journal exercises, and writing a short letter to Jesus that reflects one's spiritual labors over the month, you may be surprised at the positive response priests will give to individuals who are serious about their spiritual lives.

Working the Charts

The weeks in preparation for the Whole-Life Confession are filled with opportunities for individuals to write out many different elements that comprise their life narrative. The initial review and analysis of the charts in preparation for their Whole-Life Confession should not be the last. Encourage people to revisit those charts at least once a month.

They will, from time to time, gain new insights and see new things to add. They will also have "eyes to see" more of the connections between the persons, events, vices, sins, and so forth that they documented. Awakening is gradual, and lifelong. Encourage people to take advantage of the work they put into those charts. The spiritual fruit will be abundant. They will be startled by insights into their life and the actions of both God's grace and the enemy of human nature!

Narcissism: Passive and Aggressive

Many people have told us that the definitions and the charts of Passive and Aggressive Narcissism have changed their lives. Pride is THE Original Sin, and Narcissism is its manifestation.

Work hard to help individuals take the time necessary to properly identify the primary manifestation of narcissism in their lives as passive or aggressive. We live in a culture that celebrates human pride. If individuals are ever to grow spiritually, pride and its narcissistic face must be unmasked for the sin that it is, and identified as a spiritual cancer that only God's grace can uproot from our thoughts, words and deeds.

Evil is intelligent and has sought to destroy humanity since the very dawn of time. We cannot underestimate its powers of seduction or its full commitment to destroy humanity through the Original Sin's evolution in history. Honestly identifying one of

Original Sin's main signatures in our own history is very important for Christian growth and spiritual discernment.

Let people know that both Passive and Aggressive Narcissism are negative and neither is better than the other. But in our personality, one variety will manifest more than its counterpart. It all depends on how our personal history has unfolded.

It is possible that people will share some qualities from both of Narcissism's faces, but one will predominate. And as with all sin, especially this form of sin which is most deeply rooted in our lives, it takes God's grace to understand it and awaken to it. So if someone is having a hard time figuring it out which face of narcissism is their *go-to sin*, tell them to bring it to prayer and ask God's grace to "see, feel and touch" narcissism's manifestation in their lives.

God will answer that prayer! Sometimes the inability to discern which form of narcissism is unique to one's life simply means a person has little conscious awareness of themselves. Sometimes it means they are struggling to find the "less-embarrassing" face of narcissism (remember that *neither* is better than the other!) And sometimes it can be that they fear grappling with sin's presence in their lives.

Why? Because honestly naming narcissism's face in my story invites me to action. People may not desire to act and you cannot force them to name a form of narcissism. Be careful how you lead people here. All you can do as a leader is to invite reflection, and work hard to honestly name your own narcissism.

 C8

THE SCHOOL OF DISCERNMENT

The Necessity of Spiritual Discernment

This section is focused on the theory aspects of discernment. It is meant to help you as leaders personally improve in spiritual discernment, and to become better teachers of discernment. To become mature in discernment, one must first *truly believe* in the spiritual world, and believe in the struggle for good and evil that plays out in the human heart, in society and in history. Engaging the struggle between good and evil is the fundamental condition Christ holds forth to anyone wishing to be a disciple of His after he utters the first prediction of His passion:

> Then he said to all, "If anyone wishes to come after me, he must deny himself and take up his cross daily and follow me. For whoever wishes to save his life will lose it, but whoever loses his life for my sake will save it. What profit is there for one to gain the whole world yet lose or forfeit himself? Whoever is ashamed of me and of my words, the Son of Man will be ashamed of when he comes in his glory and in the glory of the Father and of the holy angels. Truly I say to you, there are some standing here who will not taste death until they see the kingdom of God." (Lk 9: 23-27).

This struggle was something St. Ignatius only became aware of mid-way through his life. It is worth taking some extra time to get our hearts and minds around the spiritual world so we can follow Christ daily as disciples and help others do the same. And at the heart of the spiritual world is the reality that both God and evil are real powers. We have the freedom to choose which power—which voice—we open our hearts and minds to on a daily basis. Both powers act upon us all throughout our lives. Each power has an ultimate endgame for our life: one for blessing and life; the other for curse and death (Dt 30: 19).

You, as a spiritual guide, must discover the "fact" of these personal, spiritual powers in your own life if you hope to effectively communicate their truth to others.

Ignatius was graced to discover the world of spiritual discernment as his conversion unfolded. No one can get very far in the Christian life without the benefit of spiritual discernment. The practice of an *Examen* <u>demands</u> one be a spiritual discerner. In making the *Examen* accessible, it was vital to render the discernment rules of St. Ignatius accessible to the average Catholic.

That is why *Sacred Story* adapts and rewrites these principles in a narrative format. We hope these vital guidelines for the spiritual life can find traction in this new format with those you are leading through *Forty Weeks*. With your input and ideas, we will continue to refine these tools of discernment.

The durability and practicality of Ignatian Spirituality is linked to its perfect alignment with the classic conversion. The *General Examen* of Ignatius' Spiritual Exercises targets manifest sins to secure the foundation of the conversion process. Continuing this focus, St. Ignatius' Rules for the first stages of the conversion process help the convert navigate the cross-pressures of temptation and the deception of *the dark night of the senses* that occur when mastering manifest sins.

The *Particular Examen* is tied to targeting the root sin from which all the others emerge. Unless mastered (or at least honestly identified), this root sin will undermine the entire conversion process and result in what is known as a "failed purgation."

The Rules for the second stage of the conversion process help the convert navigate the subtleties of temptation at this more foundational, root level in the conversion process. These temptations manifest themselves during the targeting of the Original Spiritual Sin at the core of one's identity and they are the *dark night of the spirit*, which is simply a way of saying that the false identity we have built in our seeking to be autonomous from God is collapsing.

We literally no longer know *who we are* and so we must be born from above to find our *true identity* in Christ. In his Autobiography, St. Ignatius describes this as a time when he felt like a schoolchild under a teacher's guidance.

It is worth pointing out to those who seek mystical awakening that there is no short cut. For true awakening to occur, some unpleasant realities must be faced and faced often! St. Ignatius' mystical experiences only emerged after the collapse of his egoistic pride and his total surrender of his life to Christ (signified in his ceasing the habit of re-confessing his past sins). It is the tipping point in Ignatius' conversion and had it not happened, he might never have become a saint.

All these ideas are explained in greater detail in *Sacred Story: An Ignatian Examen for the Third Millennium.* It is essential that all *Forty Weeks* group leaders understand these concepts so they can better appreciate the "structure" of the classic conversion process.

The dual goal of St. Ignatius' spiritual disciplines is to master our ego (narcissism, and the root sin of pride it signifies) and to make our hearts docile to God's inspiration. In recent years, self-centered spiritualties that do little but massage our egos have flourished. Dietrich Bonhoeffer describes these forms of spirituality (many identifying as Christian or Catholic)as forms of "cheap grace:"

Cheap grace means the justification of sin without the justification of the sinner. Grace alone does everything they say, and so everything can remain as it was before. 'All for sin could not atone.' Well, then, let the Christian live like the rest of the world, let him model himself on the world's standards in every sphere of life, and not presumptuously aspire to live a different life under grace from his old life under sin....Cheap grace is the grace we bestow on ourselves. Cheap grace is the preaching of forgiveness without requiring repentance, baptism without church discipline, Communion without confession.... Cheap grace is grace without discipleship, grace without the cross, grace without Jesus Christ, living and incarnate.

Costly grace is the treasure hidden in the field; for the sake of it a man will gladly go and self all that he has. It is the pearl of great price to buy which the merchant will sell all his goods. It is the kingly rule of Christ, for whose sake a man will pluck out the eye which causes him to stumble, it is the call of Jesus Christ at which the disciple leaves his nets and follows him.

Costly grace is the gospel which must be sought again and again and again, the gift which must be asked for, the door at which a man must knock. Such grace is costly because it calls us to follow, and it is grace because it calls us to follow Jesus Christ. It is costly because it costs a man his life, and it is grace because it gives a man the only true life. It is costly because it condemns sin, and grace because it justifies the sinner. Above all, it is costly because it cost God the life of his Son: "ye were bought at a price," and what has cost God much cannot be cheap for us. Above all, it is grace because God did not reckon his Son too dear a price to pay for our life, but delivered him up for us. Costly grace is the

Incarnation of God. [13]

Ignatius dismissed many highly talented men from the Society who displayed little interest in the mortification of spirit that he believed necessary for growth in spiritual maturity. It was a humble and obedient spirit that Ignatius saw as the vital quality for membership in the Society of Jesus. [14] We can intensify the Magis, the *greater good,* accomplished by individuals and institutions when we recover this goal of Ignatian Spirituality: when we recover the costly grace it requires for true spiritual maturity, illumination and cultural transformation. Doing so will aid our pastoral work and assist those with whom we work discover their Christian mission in life.

The Relational Model (Relational Paradigm)

In support of the *Forty Weeks* discernment mission, we created an easily intelligible framework. It helps to explain God's gift of our creation, sin's corrosion of the gift, and Christ's restoration of what was lost. Finding new ways of presenting the core truths of Christianity is particularly urgent today as the culture trends away from the Judeo/Christian tradition that has historically shaped Western societies. The philosopher Charles Taylor describes the scope of this divergence when he says, "the present condition of belief and unbelief can't be described purely in terms of élite

---

[13] See, Dietrich Bonhoeffer, *The Cost of Discipleship* (New York: Touchstone, 1995), 45-49.

[14] "It is in its obedience, above all, that the Society of Jesus should be distinct from other religious families. One need only recall the letter of Saint Ignatius, where he writes: "We can tolerate other religious institutes outdoing us in fasting and in other austerities that they practise according to their Rule, but it is my desire, dear brothers, that those who serve the Lord our God in this Society be outstanding in the purity and perfection of their obedience, the renunciation of their will, and the abnegation of their judgment". (Letter to the Jesuits of Portugal [26 March 1553], § 2 (MHSI 29, 671). It is to the obedience of the *Suscipe* that Saint Ignatius looked in order to highlight what it was that gave the Society its distinctive difference." *Jesuit Life and Mission Today: The Decrees & Accompanying Documents of the 31ˢᵗ—35ᵗʰ General Congregations of the Society of Jesus* (St. Louis: Institute of Jesuit Sources, 2008), 740. Cited hereafter as, "Decrees."

culture. One of the important events of the twentieth century is that the nova (of unbelief) has come to involve whole societies. It has become the 'super-nova.' "[15]

Pope Benedict engaged the Society of Jesus in its most challenging mission to date when he asked Jesuits to find effective means of evangelizing while remaining faithful to the Church's Traditions.[16] To address this mission, *Forty Weeks* proposes a relational model or paradigm to consider God as Trinity and the relational world God created.

The doctrine of the Trinity first appears in a creedal formula around 270 AD. It took this long to <u>hear</u> what *Scripture* proposes and for *Tradition* to understand and <u>teach</u> this truth. It is a foundational creed of Christianity and absolutely indispensable for understanding God, ourselves and the cosmos. Using a relational model for evangelizing and reflecting on the doctrine of the Trinity and all of creation also helps us in our discernment. Not surprisingly, it is a relational model that Pope Francis

---

[15] Charles Taylor, *A Secular Age* (Cambridge, MA: The Belknap Press of Harvard University Press, 2007), 412.

[16] "All the same, while you try to recognize the signs of the presence and work of God in every part of the world, even beyond the confines of the visible Church, while you endeavour to build bridges of understanding and dialogue with those who do not belong to the Church or who have difficulty accepting its position and message, you must at the same time loyally fulfill the fundamental duty of the Church, of fully adhering to the word of God, and of the authority of the Magisterium to preserve the truth and the unity of the Catholic doctrine in its totality...As you well know because you have so often made the meditation "of the Two Standards" in the *Spiritual Exercises* under the guidance of St. Ignatius, our world is the stage of a battle between good and evil, with powerful negative forces at work...This is why I have asked you to renew your interest in the promotion and defense of the Catholic doctrine 'particularly in the neuralgic points strongly attacked today by secular culture,'...The issues, constantly discussed and questioned today, of the salvation of Christ of all human beings, of sexual morality, the marriage and the family, must be deepened and illumined in the context of contemporary reality, but keeping the harmony with the Magisterium, which avoids creating confusion and bewilderment among the People of God." "Decrees", 823-4. The General Congregation responded positively to this invitation: "The 35th General Congregation expresses its full adherence to the faith and the teaching of the Church, as they are presented to us in the intimate relationship that unites Scripture, Tradition, and the Magisterium. The 35th General Congregation calls all Jesuits to live with the great spirit of generosity that is at the center of our vocation: "to serve as a soldier of God beneath the banner of the Cross...and to serve the Lord alone and the Church his spouse under the Roman Pontiff, the Vicar of Christ on earth." Ibid., 729-30.

highlighted when he described creation and the Church as a "love story."[17]

The Primacy of the Spiritual over Bodily Nature

We can assert from our Judeo-Christian tradition the primacy of the spiritual in the created universe. But we should begin to expand our understanding of what this means in light of our knowledge today. The advent of neuroscience and brain mapping has shown that mental processes (spiritual energy) can rewire neural networks. Strong spiritual experiences can also repair neural networks. The fact of the placebo and nocebo effects reveals that mental/spiritual thought has profound impact on the physical nature of persons, creating both health and sickness—by thought alone! Quantum theory (mechanics) has also revealed the universe as "mental and spiritual." See Richard Conn Henry's article from NATURE (Richard Conn Henry "The Mental Universe," Nature 436, no. 29, July 7, 2005). The ancient formula for sins in "thoughts, words and deeds" and their impact on our own human nature, other's human natures and nature itself, takes on a profound new meaning in light of this mental and spiritual universe. We are beginning to understand the scope of this relational universe and how our interactions with It (good or evil) can change it—even by mere thought or observation.

Scripture's most concise definition for God is in 1 Jn 4:8: "God is Love." Love, in essence, is <u>relational</u>. Thus, the Father who is Love, speaks His <u>Word</u> (*In the beginning was the Word, and the Word*

---

[17] "The Church, he said, is 'something else.' The disciples do not make the Church – they are the messengers sent by Jesus. And Christ was sent by the Father: 'The Church begins there,' he said, 'in the heart of the Father, who had this idea . . . of love. So this love story began, a story that has gone on for so long, and is not yet ended. We, the women and men of the Church, we are in the middle of a love story: each of us is a link in this chain of love. And if we do not understand this, we have understood nothing of what the Church is.' " http://www.news.va/en/news/pope-francis-church-is-in-a-love-story

was with God, and the Word was God. Jn 1:1) who is a completely unique Person but akin to the Father (*Jesus cried out and said, "Whoever believes in me believes not only in me but also in the one who sent me, and whoever sees me sees the one who sent me.* Jn 12: 44-45).

And the Love of the Father for the Son and the Love of the Son for the Father is <u>fruitful</u>. The fruit of their reciprocal Love is the Spirit, distinct and unique and like unto Father and the Son (*But when he comes, the Spirit of truth, he will guide you to all truth. He will not speak on his own, but he will speak what he hears, and will declare to you the things that are coming. He will glorify me, because he will take from what is mine and declare it to you. Everything that the Father has is mine; for this reason I told you that he will take from what is mine and declare it to you.* Jn 16: 13-15).

LOVE gives and LOVE receives amongst three distinct Persons. The "formula" for the Trinity (the three-in-one and the one-in-three) can be viewed either as an intellectual conundrum and unsolvable mystery or as the obvious expression of God's being: God is LOVE, and LOVE is *the* principle of Unity in the Trinity, and LOVE is also the prime force in the created universe. The latter is both true and easily intuited by the human heart. God, the Church and the universe are truly, as Pope Francis describes them, "a love story."

Human persons are made in the image and likeness of God (Gn 1:27). Tradition asserts that God "willed" human nature—the human person—to be unity of body and spirit.

✠ God created the human person with the capacity to love and to relate with God, whose essence is Love.

✠ The relationship that maintained our original perfection was the human person totally obedient and open to God's Love.[18]

✠ The human person's perfect *unity of body and spirit* is held in original perfection by the heart's complete obedience and openness to God's Love.

✠ Distinct persons, *unique unto themselves*, can be totally open to their mutual giving and receiving of love because of their hearts' complete obedience and openness to God's Love.

✠ Human persons, *distinct in their masculinity and femininity,* are held in original perfection by their hearts' complete obedience and openness to God's Love and in this, are able to "be fruitful and multiply" (Gn 1:28), akin to the fruitfulness of the Trinity.

✠ Human persons, individually and collectively, by their total obedience and openness to God's Love can enjoy, participate in and use—with complete harmony between themselves and the natural world—all of creation's gifts.

All is held firm and inviolate because God enabled human nature—enfleshed spirit—to participate in the life of God who is Love. The perfect balance of our spiritual and physical nature *that created the condition of immortality* required our complete spiritual unity with God. It required an undivided heart that was anchored in God alone. When we made the choice to listen and follow the voice of the one St. Ignatius calls the "enemy of human nature," our hearts were divided, and *all relationships were sundered.*[19]

---

[18] Remember, the Latin root of the word "obey" means "to listen deeply." Thus, a heart "obedient" to God is <u>a heart that listens only to God.</u> The world of the divided and broken heart—the world that Original Sin wrought—appears when human persons listened to another voice, and followed that voice instead of God alone. "Teacher, which commandment in the law is the greatest?" He said to him, "You shall love the Lord, your God, with all your heart, with all your soul, and with all your mind." (Mt 22: 36-37).

[19] But even in the profound rupture of relationships occasioned by the advent of Original Sin in human history, we are still one by virtue of our creation "through whom and for whom" all that is

Original Sin and the Rise of Two Diversities

When our primordial parents renounce their exclusive relationship with God in favor of autonomy from God, the sacred diversity of human beings as distinct persons *unified* by God's Love "falls" and becomes a twisted imitation of the original gift. This is why we call Original Sin, "The Fall" from grace (or the Fall

---

Pope Francis on Choosing "Francis of Assisi" as his Name

Some people wanted to know why the Bishop of Rome wished to be called Francis. Some thought of Francis Xavier, Francis De Sales, and also Francis of Assisi. I will tell you the story. During the election, I was seated next to the Archbishop Emeritus of São Paolo and Prefect Emeritus of the Congregation for the Clergy, Cardinal Claudio Hummes: a good friend, a good friend! When things were looking dangerous, he encouraged me. And when the votes reached two thirds, there was the usual applause, because the Pope had been elected. And he gave me a hug and a kiss, and said: "Don't forget the poor!" And those words came to me: the poor, the poor. Then, right away, thinking of the poor, I thought of Francis of Assisi. Then I thought of all the wars, as the votes were still being counted, till the end. Francis is also the man of peace. That is how the name came into my heart: Francis of Assisi. For me, he is the man of poverty, the man of peace, the man who loves and protects creation; these days we do not have a very good relationship with creation, do we? He is the man who gives us this spirit of peace, the poor man ... How I would like a Church which is poor and for the poor! *(March 16, 2013 comments to the media in the Paul VI Conference Hall).*

---

exists. In the book, *Diary of A Country Priest*, the Curé tells a distraught woman: "I don't suppose if God had given us the clear knowledge of how closely we are bound to one another both in good and evil, that we could go on living." Georges Bernanos: *Diary of a Country Priest* (Carroll and Graf: New York, NY, 2002) 166.

from Love). The Original Sin of living autonomously, and the *fallen* human nature it creates, gives rise in history to profane diversity, profane culture and profane evolution.

Autonomous individuals assert their own truth, create their own identities and thus become "like gods." The serpent spoke a partial truth when he said they would become like gods, "knowing good and evil." Autonomy from God makes them know the "good" they lost (the ability to be loved and affirmed in one's uniqueness can't be experienced in autonomy from God) and the "evil" that is autonomy's fruit (the competition, hatred and violence that separation from God creates).

In a world that evolves under the spirit of autonomy—the spirit of human nature's enemy—all relationships will ultimately be sundered. But the temptation to view autonomous living as empowering, ennobling, glamorous and acceptable continues to allure, even when its manifest fruits are infidelity, isolation, despair, violence, greed, war and death. When we renew our baptismal promises each year, we promise to "reject the glamour of evil." Popular culture depicts autonomy from the strictures of religious law as "glamorous": the icon of autonomy is to not let anyone else *tell you what to do*.

Autonomy from God inaugurated the division of the human heart. This broken and divided heart initiates a linked cataclysm of all broken relationships. Original Sin's self-assertion and self-love poisons human nature and the natural environment itself. Human nature, held immortal by the utter innocence and obedience of the persons in relationship to God's Love, is abruptly and tragically subject to spiritual, psychological and physical death.

The spirit or soul of the human person is divided. Our lower appetites battle our higher spiritual nature for supremacy (*More tortuous than anything is the human heart, beyond remedy; who can understand it*? Jer 17: 9). We can even envision how sin's devastation to our spiritual, psychological and physical nature also corrupted life at the genetic, molecular and cellular level in human persons.

The perfection in the relationship between male and female is broken. They have lost their innocence *and* the mastery over their bodies. They cover their nakedness out of personal shame (Gn 3: 7). They are ashamed because in their loss of control over their physical nature, each knows that the *other* is aware of the self-centered *objectification of the other* initiated by autonomy from God.

The Blessed Mother and Freedom from Original Sin

Classical Catholic theology has viewed Mary's freedom from the stain of Original Sin from her first moments of life (the Immaculate Conception) as preparation for her "yes" to God's plan. This allowed her to be a pure vessel for the Son of God to be born of human flesh. We might expand our understanding of what it means to be free from the stain of Original Sin. It would certainly mean total integrity of Mary's spiritual, psychological and physical being. But we can posit too that she is free from any genetic and cellular deformities caused by Original Sin's evolution through the human family. Jesus, *incarnate* as the Son of God, is completely united with his perfect bodily nature. In this he manifests the perfect union of spirit and body that God *willed* for us at the dawn of our creation and which He has won back for us by his life, death and resurrection.

The broken innocence between the woman and the man will spread in the family and into all relationships in the family of humankind. We see this allegorically in the murder of Abel by Cain, foreshadowing all future fratricide, genocide and war. We see it allegorically in the sexual subjugation and violence that evolves between the genders (Gn 6:1-4).

The fracture radiates out in humankind's interaction with creation. With the human persons broken within their very being, their relationship with the gift of creation in the natural world is broken. The Tower of Babel is an allegory of the folly caused when society seeks to create *progress* completely autonomous from God.

The allegory foreshadows all future technological and environmental overreach due to human hubris, selfishness and greed. Separated from God, humankind is blinded to creation's gift. And as we lost control over our human nature, we also lose control over our proper use of creation according to God's design. The enemy of human nature sought the death of the persons made in God's image and likeness. The enemy could also foresee human hubris, selfishness and greed destroying and poisoning the sources of life in food and water, plant and animal, required for human survival.

The Son's mission of redemption is to repair the damage of sin and death. He enters into *relationship* with humanity—a new Covenant—by being born in time and history *of human flesh*. He must repair the damage done to human nature by the choice of autonomy from God.

So we are ambassadors for Christ, as if God were appealing through us. We implore you on behalf of Christ, be reconciled to God. For our sake he made him to be sin who did not know sin, so that we might become the righteousness of God in him. (2 Cor 5: 20-21)

The Relational Paradigm and Ignatian Discernment

In offering a self-guided prayer method that incorporated lessons in spiritual discernment, it was essential to help practitioners define the parameters of right and wrong in human thoughts, words and deeds. This goal is specifically addressed in a short section of *Sacred Story: An Ignatian Examen for the Third Millennium*, titled "The Boundaries of Ignatian Discernment." The *Sacred Story* restatement of St. Ignatius' "spiritual consolation" as "Divine Inspiration," and "spiritual desolation" as "counter-inspiration," fits precisely into our post-Original Sin relational model or paradigm. Divine Inspiration is what moves one to render obedience to God and to one's authentic human nature. Counter-inspiration is what moves one to be disobedient to God and one's authentic human nature.

All inspirations <u>to live autonomously</u>, apart from God, originate from the enemy of human nature and result in the loss of faith, hope and love. Life lived autonomously will continue the rise of the profane diversity, profane culture and profane evolution that has fractured all relationships. All inspirations <u>to live in communion with God</u> (in the Church) originate from the Divine-Inspirer and result in an increase in faith, hope and love. Life lived in communion with God advances sacred diversity, sacred culture and sacred evolution. This is the holy path inaugurated at the Sinai Covenant, advanced through the Chosen People and fulfilled in the birth, life, death and resurrection of Christ Jesus. The call to communion is summarized in the command to "Love the Lord your God with all your heart, with all your soul and with all your mind." (Dt 6:4-5)

Ultimately there are only two trajectories in life—movement towards God or away from God. Spiritual discernment and its guidelines are intended to help one interpret all of one's thoughts, words and deeds, understanding which trajectory they are aligned towards. Read the lesson for Week 31 again and seek to understand Ignatius' Rules as guidelines for understanding the difference between sacred and profane diversity in human nature and social evolution—in all thoughts, words and deeds.

This does not mean that we are either all good or all bad. It means that living with our hearts divided by Original Sin, we are either moving our lives in a trajectory towards God or a trajectory away from God. Help your group to understand, just as Ignatius gradually understood, that there are only two possible "narratives" for one's life: life with God or life apart from God. This will help them sift their daydreams, definitions of success and the many desires of daily life, by seeing all these things in one of two categories: moving one towards or away from God. This framework helps participants better attune to the spiritual world and the discernment of spirits they will need for authentic spiritual growth.

The Enemy of Human Nature

Pope Francis has surprised some by affirming that there is an evil being called The Devil. Many no longer believe this to be true. Despite this trend, it is ironic to consider how many thinkers have proposed that perhaps evil works best when people do not believe in "actual evil." Google's first company slogan was, "Don't Be Evil." Eric Schmidt, Google's CEO, said recently in an NPR interview: "When I showed up, I thought this idea was the stupidest rule ever, because there's no book about evil except, maybe, you know, the Bible or something." [20]

At the heart of the deceptions in the garden was the temptation to rewrite the laws of creation and human nature. In that deception are the seeds for the destruction of God's children and the natural world.[21] Many Roman Catholics no longer believe in the existence of intelligent evil (traditionally known as the devil). My research with the Sacred Story Institute has confirmed this,

---

[20] http://www.npr.org/2013/05/11/182873683/google-chairman-eric-schmidt-plays-not-my-job

[21] If you have not seen the movie, *The Devil's Advocate*, it is worth watching. It is a good portrayal of how the enemy of human nature manifests human choice to disconnect from God's laws and its ramifications in culture. Here is a short clip from the movie's climactic scene: https://www.youtube.com/watch?v=jARp24AJWLk (Note: This is an R rated film).

although it was only a slight surprise. Even in a modern Supreme Court statement we have a striking modern day manifestation of the enemy of human nature's tempting offer in the Original Sin.[22]

Recall the film, "The Exorcist" (1973). When the Harvard trained psychiatrist Fr. Damien Karras SJ is asked by Chris MacNeil how she could get an exorcism for her daughter Regan, he replies that he would have to get her in a time machine and transport her "back to the 16th century." We have become accustomed to seeing evil only from a scientific perspective, convinced we can find "natural" causes *and cures* for all human misbehavior and sickness.

We must affirm the devil exists, but it is more important to focus on this being's *goals* rather than the entity itself. In this context, the Holy Spirit gave St. Ignatius a brilliant insight to define Satan as *the enemy of human nature*.

Satan seeks to destroy all Divinely created relationships, both in human nature and in the natural world. In the Genesis story, Satan downplays the risk involved in turning from God and *true relationship*. He inspires self-love (*You will be like gods, who know good and evil.* Gn 3: 5) so our first parents can imagine life apart from God as beautiful and safe (*You certainly will not die!* Gn 3: 4).

With the Original Sin's loss of innocence and the intimate knowledge of God, evolution is split in two. There is an evolutionary strand of grace, life and blessing—true relationship, and the work of Redemption that will bring about a new heaven

---

[22] In the 1992 Supreme Court case, "Planned Parenthood v. Casey" we read: *'At the heart of liberty is the right to define one's own concept of existence, of meaning, of the universe, and of the mystery of human life.'* It is true that free-will enables individuals to define their own "truth" apart from God. But it is ironic, and a bit chilling, to hear that particular use of free will as the hallmark of liberty enshrined in a Supreme Court decision. Again, we recall Bernard Lonergan's comments about cultural decline from footnote 9.

and a new earth. There is also the evolutionary strand of evil, curse and death—all that destroys relationships, and the work of the enemy of human nature who seeks a kingdom of death and despair.

They both move forward in history intertwined in persons, social structures, the Church and in creation itself. Discernment is necessary for us to understand the two evolutionary strands in our own personal history and in the.

As culture becomes more and more profane, separated from God's laws and God's plan for humanity, human sin and dysfunction manifests in society as progress, but it is progress of a profane nature. In fact, it is leading to tragic cultural decline, as Bernard Lonergan notes, but the decline is no longer self-evident to those blind to God's truth. It is important to identify that much of what is called progress today is actually a form of evolutionary development towards our destruction—accomplished by the loss of the knowledge of God.

Satan's goal in the beginning was to destroy the beauty of God's relationships in all of creation by destroying human nature and the harmony of the natural world. The enemy's mission advances in the world today as the *true meaning* of relationship in human nature and creation is gradually estranged from the Creator's design of relationship as gift and inheritance from the Creator. Popular culture increasingly insists that there is no *truth*, no *meta-story*, and no *fixed meaning in human nature*.

We need to be on the lookout in our personal lives, in culture and in the Church as well, for the deceptive suggestion that there is no truth apart from the truth we each define on our own terms. We recall Pilate's exchange with Jesus in John's Gospel:

So Pilate said to him, "Then you are a king?" Jesus answered, "You say I am a king. For this I was born and for this I came into the world, to testify to the truth. Everyone who belongs to the truth listens to my voice." Pilate said to him, "What is truth?" (Jn 18: 37-8)

Our first parents were deceived, thinking they saw greater joy in the invitation to sever their relationship with God in favor of self-love. That sin robbed us of our immortality and opened human history to heartache, disease and death. So too today, we are *deceived* by the promise of greater joy in the invitation to sever human nature from the natural law and the *right relationships* articulated by the Commandments.

This desire to untether human nature and creation from the laws of God is how the deceiver <u>designed</u> Original Sin to "evolve" in human society. This is a malicious, devious and intentional plan to destroy humanity and creation. We must wake up to this fact anew in our technologically- advanced modern age. Evil is real and seeks to use human instruments to accomplish its destructive goals.

To live apart from God and God's laws—the Original Sin—is today often viewed in the profane diversity of our cultural decline as enlightened, glamorous, sophisticated, and courageous. This "rush to redefine" encompasses human nature. But it also includes our relationship with the natural world as we seek to manipulate, often with unforeseen but disastrous consequences.

More and more, the glamor of evil is the seductive call to reshape human nature and the natural world according to the whims of profane human appetites. There is an important connection to John's Gospel referencing the Holy Spirit as the *Spirit of Truth*.[23]

---

[23] This phrase appears nowhere else in the Scriptures. John also uses the word "Paraclete" for the Spirit. The Jesuit Scripture scholar, Rev. Felix Just, indicates the Spirit/Paraclete's role is multidimensional. Notes of Fr. Just, SJ on Spirit in John's Gospel:

✠ As a *companion*, to be with the disciples "forever," after Jesus is gone (14:16-18; cf. 1 Jn 3:24; 4:13)

✠ As a *teacher*, who will "remind" the disciples of Jesus' own words and teachings (14:26)

We can see the Spirit's multifaceted role as the *comforting* Love and presence of God (Father and Son) who *teaches* the Church what is true about LOVE (God) and true about love (relationship) in a world that is blinded by sin to both <u>truth</u> and <u>true love</u> (true relationship).

The world is blinded because *the enemy of human nature* continues to deceive about truth and love. This is the enemy of human nature who is anti-Love/anti-Christ: *He was a murderer from the beginning and does not stand in truth, because there is no truth in him. When he tells a lie, he speaks in character, because he is a liar and the father of lies.* (Jn 8:44) The world must be constantly reminded and taught by the Spirit of Truth about true love and true relationship: *And when he comes he will convict the world in regard to sin and righteousness and condemnation: sin, because they do not believe in me; righteousness, because I am going to the Father and you will no longer see me; condemnation, because the ruler of this world has been condemned.* (Jn 16: 8-11)

Christ and His Church are the cure, guaranteed to prevent evil's planned destruction of humanity and creation initiated with the Original Sin. We must courageously reject the assertion that there is no such thing as an enemy of human nature who has launched a sinister, deliberate and intelligent plan to destroy humanity and the natural world. We must resist, because evil's only means to accomplish that plan is through human cooperation.

✠ As a *legal witness*, who will give "testimony" to the disciples and the world about Jesus (15:26)

✠ As a *judge*, who will "convict" (or "convince"?) the world "about sin and righteousness and judgment" (16:8-11)

✠ As a *revealer*, who will "guide" the disciples to the "truth" about God and Jesus (16:13-15; cf. 1 John 5:6-8)

See: http://catholic-resources.org/John/Themes-Spirit.htm for Fr. Just's full explanation of *Spirit* in John's Gospel.

Let us be clear: there _is_ an enemy of human nature and his plan is strategic, deceitful, and designed with maximum malice for God's children and creation. We have no hope for rescue from this vicious evil apart from God's power to save us. We have no hope

---

Pope Francis on Forgiveness

"Do not forget this. God always forgives, and He receives us in His love of forgiveness and mercy. Some people say – this is beautiful – that sin is an offence against God, but it is also an opportunity: the humiliation of realising [that one is a sinner] and that there is something [exceedingly] beautiful: the mercy of God." "The Church is not an organization founded by an agreement among [a group of] persons, but - as we were reminded many times by Pope Benedict XVI - is the work of God: it was born out of the plan of love, which realizes itself progressively in history." "The Church is born from the desire of God to call all people into communion with Him, to His friendship, and indeed, as His children, to partake of His own divine life. The very word "Church", from the Greek _ekklesia_, means "convocation". God calls us, urges us to escape from individualism, [from] the tendency to withdraw into ourselves, and calls us – convokes us – to be a part of His family. This convocation has its origin in creation itself." "God created us in order that we might live in a relationship of deep friendship with Him, and even when sin had broken this relationship with God, with others and with creation, God did not abandon us. The whole history of salvation is the story of God seeking man, offer[ing] humanity His love, embracing mankind." _(Quotes from Pope Francis' Weekly Teaching in St. Peter's Square, 5-29-13)._

---

apart from God's power in Christ! If we understand evil's goal as the destruction of the natural world and humanity, we will be able to reintroduce the truth that a counterforce to the Divinity—to Love—is real!

This counterforce needs to be unmasked and confronted both at the level of individual human desiring and in society's definitions of love, progress, and advancement. The Church's mission of reconciliation and compassion requires that it hold fast to the Divinely-willed purpose of human nature and nature. But the Church also offers the hope that no matter sin's destruction, forgiveness and mercy are boundless. God will create a new heavens and a new earth.

CB

Prayer advice — 27

Whole Life confession — Possible help
For general confession 31 ff

Good advice for small groups 41 ff

Examen — Previously Relatedness 53-4
Good on journaling — Simple 57-8

ABOUT THE AUTHOR

Fr. William Watson, S.J., D. Min., has spent over thirty years developing Ignatian programs and retreats. Fr. Watson has served as: Director of Retreat Programs at Georgetown University; Vice President for Mission at Gonzaga University; and Provincial Assistant for International Ministries for the Oregon Province of the Society of Jesus. He holds Masters Degrees in Divinity and Pastoral Studies, respectively (1986; Weston Jesuit School of Theology, Cambridge Massachusetts). He received his Doctor of Ministry degree in 2009 from The Catholic University of America (Washington D.C.).

In the spring of 2011 Fr. Watson launched the non-profit Sacred Story Institute, to bring Ignatian Spirituality to Catholics of all ages and walks of life. The Sacred Story Institute is promoting third millennium evangelization for the Society of Jesus and the Church by using the time-tested *Examination of Conscience* of St. Ignatius.

Sacred Story Press
Seattle, Washington, USA
sacredstorypress.com

Sacred Story Press explores dynamic new dimensions of classic Ignatian spirituality, based on St. Ignatius' Conscience Examen in the *Sacred Story* prayer method pioneered by Fr. Bill Watson, S.J. We are creating a new class of spiritual resources. Our publications are research-based, authentic to the Catholic Tradition and designed to help individuals achieve integrated, spiritual growth and holiness of life.

We Invite Your Feedback

The Sacred Story Institute welcomes feedback on all our publications. Contact us via email or letter. Give us ideas, suggestions and inspirations for how to make better resources for Catholics and Christians of all ages and walks of life.

For bulk orders and group discounts, contact us:
admin-team@sacredstory.net

Sacred Story Institute & Sacred Story Press
1401 E. Jefferson Suite 405
Seattle, Washington, 98122

SACRED STORY
ROSARY

An Ignatian Way to Pray the Mysteries

WILLIAM M. WATSON, SJ
Art by Mary Grace Thul, OP

Coming Spring 2015 in English and Spanish